CW01670440

Edible Mushrooms

& *Other Fungi*

MICHAEL JORDAN

Edible Mushrooms
&
Other Fungi

MICHAEL JORDAN

BLANDFORD

Paperback first published in the UK 1995 by Cassell plc
Wellington House, 125 Strand
London
WC2R 0BB

Distributed in the United States by Sterling Publishing Co., Inc.
387 Park Avenue South, New York, NY 10016–8810

Distributed in Australia by Capricorn Link (Australia) Pty Ltd
2/13 Carrington Road, Castle Hill, NSW 2154

Cataloguing in publication data for this title is available from the British Library

ISBN 0-7137-2586-2

All photographs by Michael Jordan except for *Morchella vulgaris* on page 27 by Eric Soothill.

Typeset by Cambrian Typesetters, Frimley, Surrey
Printed and bound in Hong Kong by
Dah Hua Printing Press Co Ltd

Contents

This book is concerned primarily with edible species of fungi. The author and publisher wish to draw the reader's attention to the toxic nature of some inedible fungi and stress that they cannot accept responsibility for mistakes in identification. Use of an authoritative field guide, detailing inedible species, will help to avoid confusion.

Mushrooms and Toadstools: An Introduction

There is something special about roaming the autumn woods and fields in search of mushrooms and toadstools. Yet, try to define the magic and one is hard pressed! I first caught the 'bug' as a student working through the rigours of my biology degree at Brighton. We had a wonderful Welsh botany lecturer, Clifford Mortlock, who possessed an ability to communicate the lyricism of the countryside and its fruits which enthralled me. He taught me the rudiments of sorting *Boletus* from *Bovista, Amanita* from *Auricularia*. He taught me the essentials of sniffing, tasting, spitting (all good attributes of the mycophile) without making it boring or pretentious. He showed me how to take a good photograph and avoid the worst pitfalls of identification. I cherish all of it. Sadly, he died some years ago.

The magic is perhaps made up from a number of ingredients. I remember an ancient pub that I often visited, damp, grubby and happy, at the end of days spent searching for rare and wonderful species in the woods near Haywards Heath in Sussex. Above the vast and generally smoky open fireplace was, and probably still is, a quotation from Coleridge: 'I have desired, and found the best of my desires in the autumn road – the mellow winds that soothe the darkening shires, and laughter and inn fires.' I guess that sums up a good deal of it, though not all. Fungi possess their own intrinsic lure. They are esoteric in every way. They claim the most extraordinary shapes, and colours, textures and aromas. Searching them out generates its own peculiar compulsion which, until you have been hooked by it, is difficult to comprehend.

Fungus hunting today, or foraying as aficionados prefer to describe it, attracts an ever-growing band of devotees for whom the search for the good, the bad and the ugly amongst things mycological can become akin to an obsession. Those of us who choose to spend our weekends wandering the autumn woods and fields, guidebooks in hand and wicker baskets at the ready, searching for these fascinating plants can probably be separated into behavioural camps. There are the strict 'spotters' whose pursuit parallels that of the railway buff on the end of the platform at Reading or Crewe. Such mycophiles follow a litany of names and numbers, rattle off Latin nomenclature with a kind of hedonistic delight and are perennially on the look-out for the rare and mysterious specimen that has thus far eluded their search. Then there are those of us with more modest aspirations, to whom the common edible mushroom is the only familiar species and the rest represent an exciting quest into the unknown. Last but not least are those (frowned upon by the first category and held in a combination of awe and horror by the second) who narrow their focus of attention on to specimens that can be taken home and eaten. One might well make a convenient fishing analogy with the purist specimen angler, the enthusiastic coarse fisherman, and the devotee of salmon and trout for the pot.

Whatever one's preference there can be few more refreshing ways of spending a fine autumn day than wending a lazy path through mellow woods and fields picking these primitive and fascinating plants. If you are interested in the culinary appeal of fungi there is also great satisfaction in carrying home a basket full of Horse Mushrooms, or boletes or blewits safe in the knowledge that your prize has not been deluged with chemicals, nor deep frozen, nor factory processed.

It is important to appreciate that the bit of the fungus which becomes visible and which we pick, be it mushroom or puffball or bracket, is not the whole plant, only its seasonal fruit. The everyday workings of the fungus are safely tucked away below the soil surface or behind tree bark in the form of a cotton woollike mass of colourless threads called the mycelium.

One of the first questions the prospective mycophagist asks concerns the difference between mushrooms, toadstools and fungi. The short answer is that the terms are largely synonymous. In general, we are brought up to believe that mushrooms are edible and toadstools are poisonous, whilst fungi tend to be nasty things that grow under floorboards and cause building inspectors to frown severely. In reality, the first two distinctions are fairly arbitrary layman's terms and the last is a scientific tag. The group of plants to which mushrooms, toadstools, moulds and mildews belong is the Fungi (pronounced, incidentally, 'fun-jai' and occasionally spelt funghi). This is a vast and ubiquitous botanical group, one of the most primitive and ancient, yet also one of the most successful. It includes, as well as the larger forms, tens of thousands of species which are so small that they can only be seen under a microscope. They live everywhere from the bottom of the sea to the tops of mountains, and from the insides of television sets to the skin between our toes. Some, like penicillin, are beneficial to mankind, others, like aspergillus and dry rot can be immensely harmful both to our health and to our economy.

Properly, all those forms of higher fungi whose fruiting bodies take the shape of a cap on top of a stalk, the agarics and boletes, are described as mushrooms. The term toadstool is of questionable origin and almost certainly has nothing to do with croaking amphibians. It is, most probably, a corruption of the German word *Tod* meaning death, and *Stuhl* meaning seat which, in English usage, has come to mean any mushroom which does not appear regularly on supermarket shelves.

In terms of nutritional value, fungi have little to commend them. Containing few nutrients, even fewer vitamins, and consisting largely of water, we eat them mainly to satisfy the eye and the palate rather than the calorie count. There is, however, more to the attraction than this, not least the bizarre and often provocative connotations which go with the physical appearance of fungi and the rather esoteric circumstances of their emergence, be it through leaf litter, grass or tree bark. It is not surprising that through the millennia the eating of fungi has been the subject of superstitions and erroneous beliefs to an unparalleled degree. The reasons are many and diverse and, even in the light of modern rationality and scientific understanding, fungi are still the most maligned members of the plant kingdom.

Most of the lore about fungi is based on ignorance. On the whole, fungi are inoffensive plants, providing a much needed scavenging and breaking-down operation on the organic detritus of nature. They are, in company with certain bacteria, the earth's composters, and without them the planet would very soon become engulfed in the dead and dying remains of its inhabitants, animal and vegetable alike.

Our present day knowledge of fungi owes a great deal to the commitment and painstaking observation of the botanists of the

Victorian era. In particular, we must acknowledge the dedication and courage of these frontiersmen in the sampling of specimens to discover their edibility. These early fungal tasters paved the way to our confident selection of the good, the bad and the worthless. We owe a considerable debt to such pioneers as C. D. Badham, whose culinary adventures resulted in the publication of the classic reference book *Esculent Funguses of England*, and to the Reverend J. Worthington Smith, whose clerical digestive tract seems constantly to have been put at risk so that we may today enjoy its findings in the safety of hindsight.

When a species is listed in the guidebooks as being edible and good the odds are that its suitability for the pan has been determined not through some modern scientific test but by one of those redoubtable die-hards who once sampled the goods, at risk to life and limb, and passed them as fit for consumption! Conversely, when a species is listed with the cautious advice edibility unknown, the comment can generally be taken to mean that nobody has yet had the stomach to fry up a few caps and munch them or, at least, the testers have not survived to tell the tale.

If, however, the nineteenth-century botanists gave us the most recent insights into the mysteries of edible fungi, the discovery movement was begun in the west by the Greeks and Romans, although the Chinese were enjoying the delights of fungus eating thousands of years ago in the Orient. Not surprisingly, the Romans adopted a less than scientific stance towards fungus eating. In short, classical observers of matters mycological subscribed to the notion that fungi possess a unique ability to absorb properties, malignant or benign, from their surroundings. In the second century AD, the Sicilian physician and herbalist Dioscorides wrote:

> Fungi have a twofold difference; their poisonous nature depends on various causes, for either such fungi grow amongst rusty nails or rotten rags, or near serpents' holes, or on trees producing noxious fruits; such have a thick coating of mucus, and when laid by after being gathered, quickly become putrid; but others, not of this kind, impart a sweet taste to sauces.

At this juncture one might imagine that Dioscorides was about to launch into a generous review. Not a bit of it. He went on:

> However even these, if partaken of too freely, are injurious, being indigestible, causing stricture or cholera. As a safeguard, all should be eaten with a draught of olive oil, or soda and lye ashes with salt and vinegar, and a decocotion of savory or marjoram, or they should be followed with a draught composed of birds' dung and vinegar, or with a linctus of much honey; for even the edible sorts are difficult of digestion.

Fortunately, today's Italian chef slicing Ceps and Oyster Caps into a fresh salad, or shaving snowflakes of truffle over your *fettucine con funghi* insists on less draconian measures and one tends not to look for antipasti of bird droppings and vinaigrette on the menu.

So why, if so much discomfort was attached to fungus eating, did the Romans bother? It was a fad and, like most fads, people were prepared to suffer to join in the vogue. Amongst the contributory factors was sheer boredom! As the Roman Empire approached its twilight years and imperial assets were running low, a general belt-tightening exercise was demanded amongst the noble patricians. Peacocks' brains and other extravagant delicacies of flesh and fowl became frowned upon by the senate, which passed sumptuary laws banning the import and use of costly and extravagant meats. The regulations omitted, however, to include vegetables amongst proscribed indulgences and so the incorrigibly hedonistic patricians looked to the most 'whacky' vegetables they could find as a novel and entertaining diversion from their by now austere diet.

In order to protect a limited supply of raw material, the privileged immediately banned the lower orders of society from collecting and eating fungi and developed an elaborate mystique surrounding the preparation and cookery of the new vegetables. They also seem to have experimented robustly – adventures which resulted, from time to time, in disaster. They also found ample use for the more lethal species in a series of celebrated assassinations, not least of which was the demise of the Emperor Claudius at the hands of the scheming and malignant Agrippina who joined forces with his eunuch to prepare a last supper of his favourite *Amanita caesarea* laced with the juices of the death cap (*A. phalloides*).

Amanita caesarea, the most famed of the Roman mushrooms, grows in more southerly latitudes of Europe and is as firm a favourite with modern Italians as it was amongst the Roman emperors. Today, in autumn, it is a common sight in the street markets of north Italian towns such as Bologna and Alba.

The Roman passion for eating fungi has never been lost on the Mediterranean appetite and down the intervening centuries one discovers all kinds of fascinating insights into its popularity. The problem is that there has always been a price to pay for the over-casual attitude with which too many Continentals view the picking and eating of wild mushrooms. The British may be overly shy, but the Latin races tend to err on the side of complacency and even foolhardiness. In 1837 a special parliamentary bill was passed in Italy because the government had become concerned about the number of deaths resulting from the sale of fungi by undisciplined collectors and traders. The *Congregazione Speciale di Sanita* came up with a seven-point code of practice:

1 Inspectors of fungi, versed in botany, were to be appointed to attend market places with the job of inspecting all fungi displayed for sale.
2 Any fungi brought into Rome were to be officially registered and the baskets were then to be sealed up in the presence of an inspector, after which the whole day's consumption was to be delivered, under escort, to a central 'bonded warehouse' until the hour of sale.
3 The fungus market was to be set up in a specific place and hawking or marketing elsewhere in the city was forbidden under penalty of fine or imprisonment.
4 At seven o'clock in the morning the inspector was empowered to re-check all merchandise laid out for sale and was to issue a printed trading permit on payment of one baiocchio (0.2p) for every 10 lb of fungi passed for sale.
5 Permits for quantities of less than 10 lb were to be issued free of charge.
6 No stale fungi from the previous day, and no maggoty specimens were allowed and all such sub-quality material was sent under strict escort for disposal in the river Tiber.
7 Power was vested in the inspectors to fine or imprison any who contravened the regulations.

A similar system was organized in France and, to this day, a French pharmacist is required to be able to distinguish *'les champignons comestibles et veneneux'* when specimens are brought in by members of the public for identification.

The traditions of centuries and perhaps thousands of years

have given the French, the Italians, the Poles and many others an indelible love of fungus eating. Find a car parked by the side of a country lane in France during an autumn weekend and the odds are that the occupants are not indulging in a late season picnic on the verge but are out scouring the woods for delicacies. Many of the misconceptions about fungi which have become established in the British Isles have probably arisen because fungi are not traditional fare as they are in Mediterranean countries. In Britain, tradition gives fungi much more esoteric and even sinister roles: they are seen as objects of mystery, superstition and evil purpose. The British will merrily select sloes and blackberries from the hedgerow whilst deadly nightshade, purging buckthorn and spindle tree offer their tempting but perilous fruits alongside, yet will shun a much smaller risk emerging from the woodland floor. Some people have argued that this attitude comes from the distant Celts and their Druidic priests, but in truth we really do not know what has created this mycophobia.

The British are also conditioned to expect just one edible mushroom, that which comes in a cellophane-wrapped pack from the supermarket, suitably clean, excised at the base and precisely the right size. Thus any instinctive assessment of a fungus is based on whether it looks, feels and smells like a shop-bought mushroom. Curiously though, that yardstick has changed during even recent decades. Less than a hundred years ago one would not have expected to find the mushrooms we know today on a market stall in the Midland shires. Instead, the Wood Blewit (*Lepista nuda*) would have been displayed.

To accompany the mystique surrounding fungi a veritable manual of fallacious advice has arisen offering 'safe tests' for fungi. Most of these practical tips, alas, are worthless. The more widely reported include the following:

'Edible fungi peel whilst the poisonous varieties do not.' This assumption is quite incorrect. The common-or-garden *Agaricus bisporus* mushroom peels readily but this is a characteristic it shares with some of the most lethally poisonous fungi.

'Poisonous fungi blacken silver spoons during cooking.' Some of the most dangerous species have no effect on the colour of silver and this particular piece of wishful thinking probably arose in response to the notion that silver will draw poisonous substances to itself and absorb them. It is probably the same questionable logic that argues a fungus to be suspect if the cut flesh changes colour. The poisonous substances supposedly react to light.

'If animals have eaten a fungus it is a good indication that it is safe for human consumption.' Alas there are many poisonous fungi which can be nibbled safely by herbivores such as rabbits but which have a much more deleterious effect on, and are definitely not suitable for, human stomachs.

'Brightly coloured specimens are dangerous, particularly red ones; dull-coloured or white fungi are alright.' Sound wisdom? Decidedly risky. One of the most poisonous of fungi, *Amanita virosa*, is pure angelic white and is appropriately called The Destroying Angel. On the other hand, I know of mushrooms offering a range of colours from lemon yellow, to vermilion to brilliant lilac which I would consume without hesitation or adverse consequence.

So much for the fallacies. What of the facts? Yes, certain fungi are poisonous to human beings. The countryside has its heroes and its villains wherever one looks. This book contains only the edible species but anyone intending to take a responsible approach to collecting fungi for eating should, as a precaution, also familiarize themselves with the dangers, and with what to do if someone accidentally consumes a poisonous species. Perhaps the most important rule here is always to keep one specimen back for possible reference, if you have not tried the material before. If you, or anyone who is eating fungi with you, experiences strong symptoms you should go at once to a hospital casualty department (not to your local GP who will have neither the experience nor the remedies), taking some of the mushroom with you for identification.

The chances of poisoning yourself, provided you take sensible precautions, are very slight. It is essential at the outset to put the matter of edibility into proper perspective since it is undoubtedly the thought that is foremost in the minds of most people considering a venture into the woods to collect fungi for the table.

We all take reassurance from statistics, so here are a few. It is difficult to calculate just how many types of higher fungi grow in the British Isles and Europe but we may safely assume the number lies in the thousands. The total figure is, however, rather academic. Many are exceedingly uncommon and still more are sub-species or varieties which only the most highly trained mycologists can distinguish. From the viewpoint of the amateur fungus hunter there are perhaps between eight hundred and a thousand species listed in the guides, of which some four or five hundred form the 'staple stock' which one is likely to encounter and take interest in. In other words there are literally hundreds of 'little brown jobs' which are difficult to tell apart and largely overlooked. Certainly it would be a rare and eccentric individual who chose to collect them for the pot.

The great majority of higher fungi – those which are big enough to pick, handle easily, and examine with the naked eye – are harmless if we happen to eat them. If some are not suitable for the table it is usually only because they are unpalatable. It does not imply that they contain harmful or lethal ingredients, only that they lack the qualifications of taste or texture which will allow us to turn out an enjoyable dish. By illustration, no matter how many ways one tries to cook a bracket fungus of the *Heterobasidium* genus, it will resist stubbornly and will still be tough and woody after all our efforts. Likewise the Bitter Bolete (*Tylopilus felleus*), a near-relative of the deliciously edible Cep (*Boletus edulis*), remains unpalatable literally to the bitter end. The significant message is that should the tenderfoot fungus gourmet inadvertently include one such rogue specimen with dinner the experience will be neither death, convulsions, sickness nor hallucinations. At worst the dish will be tainted with an unpleasant taste or texture. With most species the error will probably go unnoticed.

Only about fifty species are known to be poisonous and at least half of these are either extremely rare or obviously unsuitable to eat because they are too small. Within the 'poisonous' classification, a much smaller number, perhaps as few as a dozen, are labelled dangerously poisonous. Giving a species the label poisonous generally implies that consuming it will result in nausea, stomachache and vomiting, or perhaps a temporary mental disorder, but is unlikely to result in more severe complications. At the other end of the gastronomic scale, this volume lists about a hundred species which are known, by tried and tested measure, to be safe to eat.

It is also true that a large number of higher fungi have to be classed in the 'edibility unknown' category and for this reason the essential rules concerning the picking of fungi to eat need to be followed sensibly and carefully.

Having dispensed the countryside warnings, it is time to get out there and enjoy the taste and aroma of wild mushrooms. One of the delights of hunting fungi for the table is that, during the autumn months, they can be found in an infinite variety of habitats from mountain sides and moorlands, to woods, fields, riverbanks, city parks and even your own garden. But mushroom hunting need not be limited to September and October. Some species make their appearance during other seasons of the year so that edible varieties can be obtained, albeit with less frequency, through the winter, spring and summer periods.

We are so familiar with what a blackberry or a wild strawberry looks like that we are unlikely to confuse it with any other wild fruit in the hedgerow. It is an experience that we have gained from childhood and we are experts. But the same expertise is not available to most of us when it come to wild fungi. Few of us will have the recollection of our mothers taking us out into the autumn woods and collecting Ceps or Oyster Caps. So we need to learn from someone who knows. The guidebook is not always a safe enough source of reference, not because the information contained there is incorrect but because we may not, as novices, translate it correctly. A fundamental stumbling block when describing and illustrating living things is that there really is no such thing as a characteristic appearance. A fungus constantly alters from the moment that the young fruiting body, or sporophore, first emerges to the time when it shrivels and disappears. Not only does the age of the fruiting body directly influence its appearance but also climatic conditions. The colour of a cap may be significantly different in dry weather from that which it displays immediately after rain or in damp conditions. Heavy rainfall may, for example, leach out colour or wash away velar patches. Decrease in humidity may change a shining and slimy cap into one which is dull and tacky. Humidity can also affect the shape of a cap; thus it may be flattened in damp conditions but funnel-shaped during drought.

There is no quick and ready solution. The important message is that the fungus hunter should be aware of these pitfalls and accommodate them when puzzling out who is who in the mycological community.

The best way to identify wild fungi is to join a fungus foray led by an expert. There is no experience quite so effective as that of being told that the specimen we have collected, peered at, sniffed, nibbled and puzzled over, is *Boletus edulis* or *Pleurotus ostreatus* and good for a wonderful meal when we get home.

Most people who lead local forays have a thorough knowledge of the species that grow in their local area and, at the end of the day's hunting, they will generally lay out all the trophies on the ground and go through them one by one explaining the characteristic features. It is a terrific way to learn and to gain confidence.

This is not to say that the guidebook can be dispensed with. It is an essential part of the mycologist's armoury and it is worth buying a good comprehensive volume with clear pictures. Again, take the advice of the experts. These are the people who will have tried the guidebooks out in the field and will know the worth of each one.

Most of the comprehensive guidebooks to mushrooms and toadstools will lay out the confusing range of fungi under headings and 'edible' will not be one of them! There are two main groups of higher fungi. The more primitive are the Ascomycetes whose spores mature within microscopic flask-shaped asci and are then shot out through the tips of these containers. They include cup fungi, morels, truffles and a range of odds and ends. The larger group, the Basidiomycetes includes all the bracket fungi and agaric or gill-bearing fungi as well as the polypores, boletes, puffballs, stinkhorns and jelly fungi. In all of these the spores are borne on the tips of microscopic projections looking like teats on a miniature cow's udder. There is something of a tradition which places the bracket fungi first in the group, small delicate brackets followed by the larger polypores. These are accompanied by the fairy clubs, hedgehog fungi and chanterelles. The section is followed by the agarics which are usually segregated according to the colour of their mature gills, classified as white (or cream), pink, chocolate and rust-coloured. The boletes are often tagged on to the end of the agaric section. The third section conventionally lists the puffballs and their allies and the final section of Basidiomycetes includes the jelly fungi.

Don't expect each specimen to come equipped with a common name. At the end of the last century there was a popular trend to tag every fungus but many of the common titles were short-lived and have been largely forgotten. Although some popular English names have stuck and become accepted in the field guides, the majority of fungi have to be remembered by their Latin names. This may seem rather daunting but it is actually quite easy once some of the genus names become familiar. The essential principle

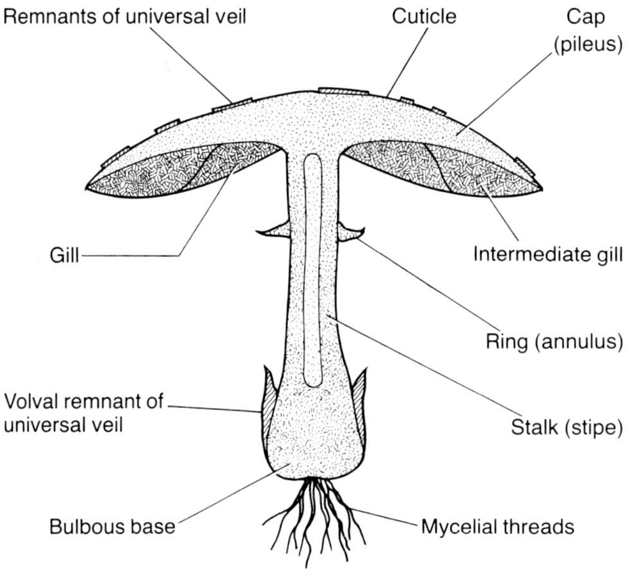

Section through a generalized agaric

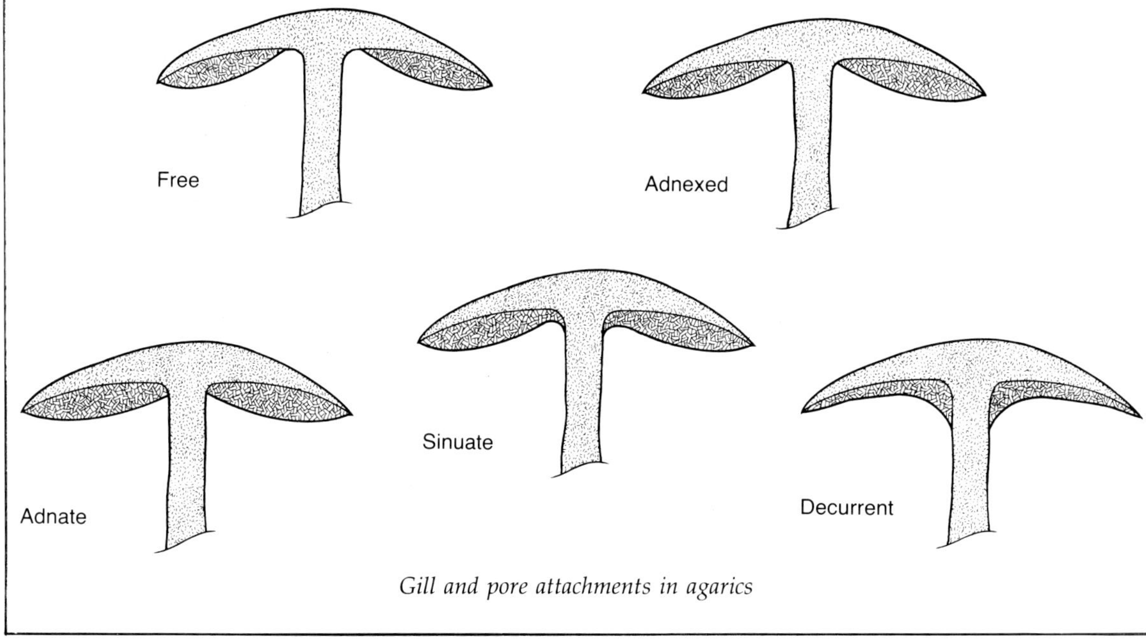

Gill and pore attachments in agarics

to remember is that each species, in common with all living things which are identified under the binomial system, will have two names, the first being the genus name, the second being the species name. Thus, for example, the so-called milk caps belong to the *Lactarius* genus and the Saffron Milk Cap is separated from all the others by its individual or specific name, *deliciosus*. The basis of mycological naming, or nomenclature, is the classic work of the botanist Elias Fries, the *Icones Selectae Hymenomycetae* compiled between 1867 and 1884. Names may subsequently have been amended, individual fungi may have been moved from one genus to another, but the groundwork is that of Fries and is usually denoted by the letters Fr. after the name of the species.

The next most important rule of fungus hunting is to remember that details matter perhaps far more than when identifying flowers. Identification often depends on quite inconspicuous details of shape, texture, colour, taste and smell. As far as possible here, the descriptions incorporate everyday English terms like velvety, hairy or mealy to describe textures but in more scientific identification the descriptions are more precise. Thus the term 'tomentose' may be found when a surface is thickly downy with soft, matted hairs, whilst 'pilose' will appear if the hairs are long and more easily visible. Thus one needs to look carefully at details and never presume identification from general appearance. The difference between a dry cap and a slimy one might mean the difference between one species and another.

The expert will probably arrive armed with a box of chemicals to rub or pipette on to mushroom flesh. Similarly, the dedicated mycologist will take specimens home and inspect the spores under a microscope. Don't worry about this. It is strictly for the advanced class and is largely unnecessary when collecting the edible specimens included in this guide. The essentials which you will need for a happy day of mushroom hunting are the book of words, a flat, open-weave basket or trug, a sharp knife, a ruler, wellies and a good warm coat. An umbrella may not go amiss either. If you really feel keen a small magnifying glass or lens can be a useful addition to your equipment.

So, in practical terms, there you are, out in the woods, and the first likely looking specimen hoves into view. What do you do? When collecting specimens, don't just rush in, grab, and move on. First of all check the surroundings. If the species you have located in the book looks like the mushroom you have just found in the depths of an oakwood, but is described as growing under conifers keep turning the pages because you are looking at the wrong one. Check if the specimen is really growing on soil or on a submerged root or piece of rotten wood. Is it growing on manure? What are the dominant trees? Is there a tree of a different kind in close proximity? Is the soil acid (often sandy) or alkaline (chalk and limestone)? All these factors can influence the selection of species which are often fussy about the habitat, the soil and the dominant vegetation. Some fungi will only grow in the company of specific kinds of tree.

Now you are ready to pick. Never listen to the so-called conservation advice that you should cut the stalk of the mushroom to avoid damaging the mycelium. For one thing this is biologically inaccurate. The damage to the underground part of the fungus is minimal when you pull up the fruiting body. More importantly though, there may be vital identification features right at the base of the stalk which may be buried some way into the ground. In short, collect the whole specimen, not just the cap with the top of the stalk. Some fungi which grow on wood may need cutting away but this is less critical for identification.

Note the diameter of the cap and check it against the description in the guidebook. Pay careful attention to colour and texture and to the presence of scales, fibres or patches. Examine the stalk and note if it has a ring or a bulbous base or any other obvious identification features. Next break a little of the flesh in the cap and decide if it is fibrous or crumbly; see if it exudes milk. Look carefully at the gills and note their colour and the way they are attached to, or free from, the stalk.

Often the guidebook will recommend that you taste a little of the flesh. There is a correct way of approaching this awesome task so that even the poisonous specimens can be sampled. Bite off a tiny portion and break it up between your front teeth and the tip of your tongue to ascertain if it is sweet, mealy, acid or bitter. Then spit out the remains without swallowing and clear your mouth. Not the most elegant of exercises, but quite safe!

Once the specimen has been correctly identified by examining all of its more obvious features, the base of the stalk which may have soil attached to it can be removed. In any case brush off any surplus debris. The instinctive way of doing this is to hold the mushroom by its stalk with the cap hanging down. Wrong! All the gritty bits which you carefully remove from the base of the stalk will find their way, with inerring certainty, into the crevices between the gills from where they are extremely difficult to extract. Keep the mushroom cap pointing upwards and clean it off from below. Then lay it, upsidedown or on its side, whichever seems convenient, in the collecting basket. Resist the temptation to pile mushrooms one on top of another. They will only be spoiled. It is better to collect a limited number of good specimens than to load the basket to the rim with everything you find when most of the material will be damaged and wasted. Never put mushrooms into polythene bags. Often wild fungi possess a higher water content than shop-bought buttons and will rapidly sweat and become mushy in the airless confines of a plastic container.

As a sound piece of general advice, no different from that if you were picking vegetables in the garden, only select mushrooms that are young, firm and healthy-looking. If you can see bore holes or they seem flabby, discard them at once. Have a good sniff at each specimen and check the description of aroma in the guidebook. If it smells in any way fishy or rotten, unless such characteristics are specifically noted, throw it out. It is past its sell-by date!

Probably the greatest risk of confusion, and the one which has claimed most victims historically, is between the genera *Amanita*, *Lepiota* and *Agaricus*, all of which include a number of species which are of comparable size and may possess certain common features. The chart overleaf, therefore, may be useful for the beginner. It is fair to say though that the distinction between the three very quickly becomes intuitive and presents no dilemma.

The fungi included in the following pages are selected from a wide range of species that are technically edible and good. I have attempted to choose species that are, on the whole, common; species that possess reasonably distinctive features; and species which should cause no problems to the most fragile of constitutions. It should be noted that some species have been placed in the list with a strict proviso. These include, for example, *Gyromitra esculenta*. There is a logic in this. Many books on edible fungi, particularly those of Continental authorship, will describe such mushrooms as a matter of course. Where a specimen, widely reported elsewhere as being good for eating, is sensibly to be treated with caution, it has been included here with appropriate comments. It is best to adopt the principle that ignorance is a poor

	Cap surface	Stalk structure	Presence of ring	Base of stalk	Gill colour	Gill attachment
Agaricus	Either smooth or scaly	Firm (white)	✓	Sometimes club-shaped or swollen	Pink or grey becoming chocolate	Typically free
Amanita	Smooth but usually with whitish patches of veil (not present in *A. phalloides*)	Firm (white)	✓	Bulbous with distinctive ridge or with remains of volval bag attached	White	Typically free
Lepiota	Generally scaly	Often hard and woody (whitish)	✓	May be swollen or bulbous	White	Typically free with gutter

defence and it is wiser, therefore, to acknowledge and detail rather than to disregard such specimens.

It should also be stressed, again, that this book contains only the edible species. Anyone who is seriously intending to collect fungi for eating should also familiarize themselves with 'the opposition'. There are a number of good field guides available and the more creditable ones will identify clearly those species which are poisonous.

The species which follow are given the Latin names generally accepted at the time of publication, followed by the common name where this exists. The reader should be aware that Latin nomenclature does change from time to time often, one suspects, on the whim of some laboratory-bound boffin, who never has to juggle with the confusion he causes to us poor amateur hunters. For example the Common Field Mushroom *Agaricus campestris* used to be known as *Psalliota campestris*. Where these archaic names may still be encountered in field guides, they have been listed under the current Latin names.

Aleuria aurantia

(Peziza aurantia)

Orange Peel Fungus

■ **Where and when** *Aleuria aurantia* grows generally in groups rather than as solitary individuals and it appears on bare soil or amongst thin grass in sheltered places around the garden. The fruiting bodies appear in autumn and may continue until early winter.

■ **Appearance** This pretty fungus belongs to the Discomycetes group, which means that the fruiting body is cup- or saucer-shaped and its spores are borne on the upper surface of the cup in microscopic flasks or asci. By far the most distinctive feature is the colour: the inside of the cup is bright orange whilst the outer surface is paler and covered with a fine white down. The cup size varies according to age but is usually between 0.5 and 10 cm across. At first the cup is deep and fairly regular in shape but as it matures the profile becomes more flattened and wavy. It has no stalk.

■ **Cookery** The taste is mildly mushroomy but there is not much body and the flesh is brittle so *A. aurantia* is to be considered more as a decorative addition to the plate than as a meal in its own right. It should be given a minimum of cooking, preferably sautéed very lightly just before addition to a dish. One of the more unusual French suggestions for this fungus is to decorate a rice pudding with the fresh caps in a gooseberry or redcurrant jelly.

Gyromitra esculenta

False Morel

This specimen is included because it may be found in a number of Continental recipe books where it is listed as edible and because it can be confused with *Morchella esculenta*. It should, however, be treated with extreme caution.

■ **Where and when** *Gyromitra esculenta* favours sandy soils and typically is found with pines or other coniferous trees.

■ **Appearance** Unlike the true morels (*Morchella* species), *G. esculenta* bears a cap which is irregular and folded into brain-like lobes rather than being pitted. The cap is generally reddish brown but can be darker date brown and it grows to between 3 and 9 cm across on a stubby pallid stalk which, when cut open, is divided into irregular chambers.

■ **Cookery** Although considered palatable in eastern Europe and other parts of the world, *Gyromitra* poisoning has been recorded regularly. The species is, according to most authorities, deadly poisonous when eaten raw and it has to be cooked in a special way. It is first boiled and the water is discarded. It is then cooked again. One of the potential dangers lies in that the toxins are not entirely eliminated by cooking and their effect may be cumulative. Poisoning results in the medical conditions of haemolytic jaundice and haemoglobinurea. Records suggest that people may have eaten the fungus regularly and suffered no ill-effects until suddenly symptoms of poisoning appear. If you discover *Gyromitra* in a cookery book, however tempting the recipe, it is best ignored. Many recipe books issue the warning that species of *Gyromitra*, along with *Helvella* species and morels, are all suspect unless picked very young because the ripe spores become toxic, but even then collection for the table is foolish.

Helvella crispa

Common White Helvella

■ **Where and when** Most of the *Helvella* fungi are considered edible. This is one of the largest and most easily spotted. It grows on soil in mixed woods, often adjacent to paths in damp areas and it makes an appearance from early summer (occasionally in the spring) through until the first frosts.

■ **Appearance** The fruiting body is whitish and distinctive. A saddle-shaped cap, cream-coloured, lobed and irregularly folded, sits on top of a white stalk, thick, irregularly ribbed and folded and punctured with cavities. The overall height of the fruiting body is up to 10 cm, of which the cap occupies about half. The fertile surface bearing the asci, or spore-containing flasks, lines the outer surface of the cap.

■ **Cookery** These fungi generate very small quantities of helvellic acid. In the raw state, the acid is actively poisonous, potentially causing the same medical conditions of haemolytic jaundice and haemoglobinurea seen in *Gyromitra* poisoning. In this and other edible *Helvella* species, however, the toxins are completely destroyed either by drying or heating the fungus in cookery. It is thus no more problematic than many of the vegetables we cook and eat without a second thought. The main provisos to collecting it for the table are that it should not be eaten raw and should be picked when young.

Helvella lacunosa

Black Helvella

■ **Where and when** This is another distinctive and edible *Helvella* species which appears during the autumn months in mixed woods, often favouring burnt ground. It is regarded as frequent rather than common in occurrence but may be overlooked because of its colour.

■ **Appearance** The fruiting body is dark greyish black, otherwise not unlike *H. crispa* though generally a little smaller, extending up to 8 cm in overall height. A saddle-shaped cap, lobed and irregularly folded, sits on a thick, ribbed and folded stalk which is of a paler grey than the cap colour. One of the cap lobes typically points upwards. The fertile surface bearing the asci lines the outer surface of the cap.

■ **Cookery** The precautions which are noted for *H. crispa* need to be applied here because *H. lacunosa* contains the same helvellic acid when it is fresh and before drying or cooking. The method of preparation and cookery is the same.

Morchella vulgaris

All the true morels (*Morchella* species) are edible and extremely good for the table.

■ **Where and when** These species tend to be more common in Continental Europe than in the British Isles. Thus *M. vulgaris* makes only an occasional appearance in England, particularly in the south where it grows in open woodland and in gardens under hedges. The morels are all vernal species, appearing in late spring.

■ **Appearance** The fruiting body can be up to 12 cm high with a conical head or cap, flesh coloured becoming paler with age, patterned with a distinctive network of pits and cavities with the fertile asci and which are separated by blunt ridges of sterile tissue. The cap sits upon a short, thick, whitish stalk. Note: *M. esculenta* can be larger, up to 20 cm high, with an ovoid or rounded profile and more acute, reticulated ridging.

■ **Cookery** Like many of their relatives, these fungi contain very small quantities of helvellic acid. In the raw state, the acid is actively poisonous, potentially causing the medical conditions of haemolytic jaundice and haemoglobinurea. The acid is completely destroyed, however, either by drying or heating the fungus in cookery. The provisos to collecting morels for the table are that they should not be eaten raw and that they should be picked young.

In certain parts of Europe morels are taken very seriously indeed. In eastern France, on the slopes of the Jura and Vosges mountains, there is a thriving cottage industry collecting and preserving morels (French: *morilles*). The fruiting bodies are threaded into long strips and hung up in the kitchens to dry. Although they shrivel to dark, unappetizing-looking lumps, after soaking overnight in water, the texture is fully reconstituted and none of the flavour is lost. Many are sold on to shops and to a substantial export market. A thoroughly versatile fungus, the morel stands as a vegetable on its own but it is best incorporated as a flavouring for soups, sauces, omelettes and pasta dishes. Probably the most exquisite tagliatelle I have ever tasted, served to me by the patron of a small restaurant in Nice, was prepared in a rich, wine-laden morel sauce and served straight from a lethally hot iron skillet.

The Italians also treat morels as a serious delicacy, cooking them by coating liberally with olive oil after first dressing with fresh mixed herbs and seasoning. The caps are then stewed with a little white wine, the mixture is thickened slightly and served with a garnish of toasted breadcrumbs and lemon.

Peziza badia

■ **Where and when** One of the commonest of the cup fungi or Discomycetes, the species grows on soil, often on or beside woodland paths and particularly favouring clay soils.

■ **Appearance** The fruiting body emerges in the shape of an irregularly flattened cup, often with a wavy margin and measuring 3–8 cm across. The colour is brown to olive brown on the upper, inner surface whilst the outer surface is reddish brown and faintly scurfy. The fertile layer of tissue bearing the asci lines the upper surface of the cup. There is no stalk.

■ **Cookery** One of the few cup fungi worth eating, *P. badia* probably needs pointing out by an expert if you do not know it already as there are a number of related species that look similar. None, however, are poisonous and if you make a mistake the only part of you that will suffer is your palate! *Peziza badia* is thin-fleshed and mild in taste. It needs the lightest of cooking.

Its value is limited to serving as a garnish or an addition to an omelette. Don't get too excited if you find any specimens.

Sarcoscypha coccinea

(Peziza coccinea)

Scarlet Elf Cup

■ **Where and when** The species appears through the winter months on pieces of dead, often buried wood, either coniferous or deciduous. Often found in small groups, it is not uncommon in Britain but is more likely to be discovered in the west of England.

■ **Appearance** This elegant cup fungus is very easy to spot because of its dramatic scarlet colour marking a countryside which is otherwise seasonally drab. *Sarcoscypha* develops into a broad cup-shape, scarlet inside and covered on the outer surface with a fine white matt of hairs. The cup margin becomes ragged with age and the cup is attached by a short stalk to the host material.

■ **Cookery** Like other cup fungi, *Sarcoscypha* is thin-fleshed and is mainly of value to decorate a dish with an attractive colour. The French recipe which used *Aleuria aurantia* to grace a rice pudding is equally applicable to *Sarcoscypha* and it is also quite acceptable and harmless to eat raw. If it is to be cooked it is best employed in sauces or omelettes where its bright colour makes a worthwhile feature.

Tuber aestivum

Summer Truffle

■ **Where and when** This species is amongst the limited number of fungi whose fruiting bodies grow partly or wholly underground and whose spores are spread by animals. Truffles rely on aroma and flavour as an attractant; when the fungus is eaten, the spores pass through the animal's digestive system and are conveniently dispersed.

Truffles are difficult to find unless you happen to own a dog or a pig with a good nose for them. In Britain *Tuber aestivum* is discovered generally on chalk and limestone soils in the south of England in beechwoods (or where beechwoods have recently existed). The fruiting bodies develop from late summer to autumn.

The best way of searching for truffles is to clear an area of ground of leaf litter: the truffles often reveal themselves as little 'volcanic mounds'. To have the best chance of seeing them you may need to get down on all fours and squint along the soil surface.

■ **Appearance** Each truffle is sub-spherical, up to 5 cm across, dark brown or black with a purplish tinge and has an irregular warty surface made up of pentagonal scabs. The fertile inner mass is a greyish cream colour, typically with a purplish tinge and criss-crossed with irregular marbling. The spores are white. The smell is not distinctive and the taste is nutty.

■ **Cookery** Not so distinctively flavoured as the Perigord Truffle (*Tuber melanosporum*) or the famed White Truffle of northern Italy (*Tuber magnatum*), the Summer Truffle nonetheless makes fine eating. It is essentially to be used as a flavouring and will enhance omelettes, soups and salads quite delightfully. Wash it well but leave the outer black surface intact without attempting to peel it, and then slice or shred over the dish. Truffle does not need cooking. It is almost impossible to describe the taste though many mycophiles have waxed lyrical in the effort to do so! Some say it approaches a nutty flavour, others that it is earthy.

Pigs were once employed to hunt for truffles, but they possess certain inbuilt drawbacks. Only female pigs are suitable and, since the aroma of the truffle is similar to that of a male pig's pheromones, they tend to become overexcited and liable to remove the fingers of the truffle hunter who is trying to retrieve his prize. In France pigs were eventually replaced by poodles, equally effective in rooting out truffles but willing to leave fingers attached whilst doing so.

The Italians treat truffle hunting as big business. The dogs employed are mainly cross-bred pointers or other retrieving hounds. It can take up to two years for a *trifolau* to train a dog and a proficient one can earn its owner thousands of pounds in a season. It is not an uncommon sight to see an elderly Fiat groaning up a country lane and then disgorging four or five large hounds which high-tail it for the woods whilst their gnarled owners follow at a more leisurely pace. In the main truffle market of Alba, a large White Truffle can change hands for several million lire.

The Romans were devotees of the truffle. The fruiting bodies were sliced, parboiled, seasoned, skewered and roasted, then marinaded in wine, honey, pepper and an extract of fish guts known as *liquamen*, which substituted for the scarce commodity of salt. The truffles were next transferred to a cooking pot, casseroled and finally served up. A simpler recipe involved cooking the truffles like a haggis, bagged up in a length of pig's gut, and roasted.

The English Victorians preferred either to roast the truffles in hot ashes, or to boil them.

Cantharellus cibarius

Chanterelle Comestible; Chevrette; Crete de Coq; Girole

■ **Where and when** Chanterelles are found typically under broad-leaved trees from summer to late autumn growing on soil. Sometimes a solitary specimen may emerge but usually the fruiting bodies are found in groups.

■ **Appearance** The fruiting body is distinctively apricot yellow all over and, although flattened with an incurved rim when young, the cap is typically funnel-shaped at maturity with a wavy, lobed margin. It can extend to 10 cm across. *Cantharellus cibarius* may possibly be confused with a species from a completely different genus of fungi, the False Chanterelle (*Hygrophoropsis aurantiaca*), which is said to be edible but has been reported to cause hallucinations in some individuals. The Chanterelle, however, is easily told apart if one looks carefully at the underside of the cap. It does not possess proper gills but rather irregularly forked narrow ridges which run steeply down the solid stem. The gills of *Hygrophoropsis*, although also forked, are straight and more orangey coloured. *Hygrophoropsis* is also limited to conifer woods and heaths. The Chanterelle has a faintly apricot smell not shared by *Hygrophoropsis*.

■ **Cookery** The Chanterelle is a true culinary delight, one of the most marvellous fungi for eating and a must for any mycological gourmet. A versatile and well-flavoured fungus which keeps its texture well during cooking, it is used in sauces and soups, as an accompaniment to meat and fish dishes, as a garnish and as a vegetable on its own or mixed with other contrasting mushrooms. It has long been popular in Italy and in France where it is known principally as La Girole. In season large quantities were once gathered from the forests around Paris and dried or pickled. Nowadays the species has become a comparative rarity there to the extent that for a number of years an unlikely export trade in *C. cibarius* has been developing: the fungi are picked and shipped to the Continent from the cultivated Scottish pine forests.

Cantharellus cibarius was once collected on a commercial scale in England, chiefly in the woods around Chelmsford in Essex, from where it found its way, not to consumers in France, but to Covent Garden market. It was on the menu at the Freemasons Tavern in London where it was traditionally served on state occasions. The fungus has a fine, distinctive, slightly peppery flavour and, whilst it is a little rubbery, this has advantage in that the fungus retains texture on cooking. One method of tenderizing, if needed, is to soak the caps in milk overnight before cooking. They can either be simmered in seasoned milk and butter or gently sautéed with a few chopped shallots.

Cantharellus infundibuliformis

(Cantharellus tubaeformis)

Chanterelle Grise

■ **Where and when** The fruiting bodies of *C. infundibuliformis* appear during the autumn months in both broad-leaved and coniferous woods, usually on acid soils. It is frequent rather than common.

■ **Appearance** Closely related to the true Chanterelle (*C. cibarius*), this species has a similar appearance though it is altogether thinner with a dull brown cap surface and 'gills'. The latter eventually turn greyish yellow. The cap extends only to about 5 cm across. The stem also tends to be more slender and grooved and is usually partly hollow. The smell is faintly aromatic but, until cooked, the taste is a little bitter.

■ **Cookery** Though not quite in the same league as *C. cibarius*, it is not unlike its more celebrated cousin and is worthwhile for cookery.

Clavulinopsis luteo-alba

(Clavaria luteo-alba)

■ **Where and when** Amongst the most delicate and attractive of fungi, this species grows mainly in short turf and moss on lawns, and appears in the form of occasional clusters of club-shaped, unbranched fruiting bodies.

■ **Appearance** Each 'club' is egg yellow with a more pallid tip. It stands up to 6 cm tall and is quite slender, sometimes with a vertical groove.

■ **Cookery** Because of its size, colour and delicacy the species is interesting as a decorative addition to a dish, perhaps scattered on a fresh salad and, in general, the edible fairy clubs can be pickled in oil. *Note*: some Continental authors advocate the use of this species whilst others suggest that its edibility is uncertain. Proceed with caution.

Clavulina cristata

(Clavaria cristata)

White Coral Fungus

■ **Where and when** The fruiting bodies often appear in patches covering an area of woodland floor during the late summer and autumn months before the first frosts under both coniferous and broad-leaved trees.

■ **Appearance** This is a delightful-looking species of the fairy coral family; it is closely related to the club fungi. Each fruiting body forms a densely branching white tuft with delicately fringed tips, growing to 8 cm in height.

■ **Cookery** *Clavulina cristata* has the same culinary appeal as the club fungi: a decorative addition to dishes, with a faintly mushroomy aroma. The treatments in the kitchen are essentially the same as those for *Clavaria argillacea*. If the fungus is to be cooked it should be given the lightest and quickest sauté.

Clavulina cinerea

(Clavaria cinerea)

Grey Coral Fungus

■ **Where and when** This species can appear in the form of a solitary tuft or in a group and is to be found in woods generally growing on the soil during late summer and autumn months. It is quite common.

■ **Appearance** Closely related to the White Coral Fungus (*C. cristata*), this species is a little larger at maturity, up to 10 cm tall, and is wholly ash grey in colour.

■ **Cookery** Its value in the kitchen is similar to that of *Clavaria argillacea*.

Clavulina rugosa

(Clavaria rugosa)

Wrinkled Coral Fungus

■ **Where and when** Typically appearing in small groups on the woodland floor, this species is fairly common from late summer to autumn.

■ **Appearance** Closely related to the White Coral Fungus (*C. cristata*), *C. rugosa* grows into more of an antler shape than a tuft, with fewer branches. It is wholly white or cream-coloured and can extend up to 12 cm in height. It gets its popular name from the wrinkled appearance of the surface of the fruiting body.

■ **Cookery** Its culinary value is similar to that of *Clavaria argillacea*.

Craterellus cornucopioides

(Cantharellus cornucopioides)

Horn of Plenty; Trompette de Mort

■ **Where and when** Related to the Chanterelle, this fungus grows in clusters on soil in deciduous woods, particularly under beech, and can appear throughout the late summer and autumn. In some areas it is quite abundant.

■ **Appearance** It appears in colours ranging from dark brown to black when wet, drying out to a pale ash grey or grey brown. The fruiting body, true to its popular name, grows in the shape of a deep hollow trumpet which flares out into a rolled back, irregular, wavy mouth. The surface has a scurfy appearance. There are no obvious gill-like ridges on the underside, although there may be shallow wrinkles. The fungus does not have a distinctive aroma.

■ **Cookery** *Craterellus* makes a popular dish on the Continent though it needs some of its natural toughness removed. It seems least popular in France where it obtains a generally low rating and is preferred, if at all, dried and powdered as a condiment or as a garnish. In Scandinavia it is traditionally given a prolonged gentle baking with butter in a casserole dish, whilst in Italy the caps are sliced thinly, boiled gently in milk, then beaten on a board and finally sautéed.

Fistulina hepatica

Beefsteak Fungus

■ **Where and when** *Fistulina hepatica* is a parasitic (on a living host) or occasionally saprophytic (on a dead or dying host) fungus which grows out from the lower trunks of broad-leaved trees and from felled logs. It causes great economic damage, mainly to oak and Spanish chestnut, although the brown-stained wood it causes has a certain aesthetic value in furniture making. The fruiting body is annual, appearing from late summer through the autumn.

■ **Appearance** A tongue-shaped member of the Aphyllophorales group of bracket fungi, *F. hepatica* possesses a dramatic appearance at maturity. The fruiting body extends up to 25 cm across, sometimes rising from a stubby stalk. In the early stages the upper surface is pink but it then alters, becoming orange red and eventually dull, dark brown in old specimens. The bracket feels rough and sometimes slightly sticky. The underside, which first appears whitish and then turns brown, is covered with a mass of pores through which the spores are discharged from minute tubes. The body is thick and fleshy and oozes a blood-red juice. There is no distinctive aroma but the juice tastes acidic.

■ **Cookery** In spite of its startling similarity to raw meat and although it is unquestionably edible, this fungus will probably disappoint the aficionado! Continental recipe books rarely mention it although I should add the caveat that such omission does not always imply criticism. I make no strong personal claims and it is not amongst my favourite fungi, but fungal gastronomes of the past have extolled beefsteak fungus as 'scarcely distinguishable from broiled meat' and 'a treat for an epicure'. Well, each to their own! The acidic flavour is largely muted when the specimen is well cooked and some people may approve of the piquancy but, as a dish, it needs to be seasoned well and jollied along with shallots and cream or whatever indulgence takes you. One other past use, which has something to recommend it, is to include slices of the young, firm flesh raw in salads. The tartness here is quite pleasant and the flavour is interesting.

Grifolia frondosa

■ **Where and when** Though this fungus is uncommon, when one does come across it, the fruiting bodies are often in large masses weighing several kilos. It emerges during the autumn months, arising from the extreme base of broad-leaved trees, particularly oak and beech.

■ **Appearance** The individual fruiting bodies are tongue- or shell-shaped and arise from a central stalk which branches repeatedly to create a colony which can extend to 40 cm across. Each cap is up to 10 cm across, olivaceous or brown, leathery and typically wrinkled. The compound stalk is cream-coloured. The fertile surface on the underside of the cap is housed inside tubes which open through fine pores, also cream. These extend typically down into the stalk zone. The spores are white. The young caps have no distinctive taste or smell but, as they mature, they acquire an aroma of mice!

■ **Cookery** Unless one selects the youngest caps, *G. frondosa* tends to be rather tough and requires long and careful cooking. Once this drawback is overcome, however, a lightly aromatic dish rewards the effort.

Hydnum repandum

Hedgehog Fungus; Pied de Mouton; Barbe de Chèvre; Langue de Chat

A very distinctive mushroom-like species whose most prominent characteristic has provided rich inspiration for a bevy of common names.

■ **Where and when** The fruiting bodies appear on soil in both coniferous and broad-leaved woodlands from late summer through the autumn period. It is quite common and may occur in small groups though it is more typically found as a solitary specimen.

■ **Appearance** Although at first glance it looks like an agaric fungus, *Hydnum* actually belongs to the Aphyllophorales group which includes the brackets, chanterelles, clubs and corals.

The fruiting body has a creamy appearance with a cap that is at first convex and then slightly depressed in the centre. The surface looks not unlike freshly baked white bread but the real identification give-away is underneath the cap where the spore-bearing layer is mounted on a forest of little spines. These may be of a slightly deeper cream than the cap colour, or even tinted salmon pink. The cap, which can measure up to 15 cm across, is mounted on a short thick stalk.

It is the spines, of course, which give the fungus many of its rather quaint animal-oriented names. Whilst in Italy it is known as Steccherino or little hedgehog, the French, for some obscure reason, prefer the title Pieds de Moutons. Throughout the Continent during the season you will regularly find *Hydnum* on sale in markets. Some people insist that the taste is reminiscent of oysters!

■ **Cookery** Culinary-wise, *H. repandum* makes a splendid dish. It possesses a slightly granular texture and a fine flavour (oysters notwithstanding). I know of a number of devotees who prize Hedgehog Fungus on a similar scale of excellence to Chanterelle and Cep. Do not be put off by the slightly bitter taste when raw: it disappears rapidly on cooking, particularly if you carry out a brief preliminary boiling and discard the water. Many chefs prefer to scrape away the spines before use. You will generally come across advice to remove them in Continental cook-books but it is not essential. As a general rule, use plenty of fluid in the preparation because *Hydnum* is otherwise rather dry. By and large, *Hydnum* is incorporated in fricassees of other fungi because its creamy colour and granular texture pair well with many other species. Don't be hesitant to use it. I know at least one top-flight London chef, who prizes it above many others.

Polyporus squamosus

Dryad's Saddle

■ **Where and when** One of the fleshy polypore fungi, this typical bracket-like member of the Aphyllophorales group grows both as a parasite (on a living host) and as a saprophyte (on a dead or dying host) of deciduous trees and felled logs. It is associated particularly with sycamore and beech where it does considerable damage by causing the rotting of the timber. The fruiting body is annual, developing from the late spring through the summer months and it is quite common. You may, however, need to look fairly high up in the living tree to spot it (and be fairly athletic to bring it down too).
■ **Appearance** The bracket first appears as a stubby, flat-tipped, 'knob' but when mature it is kidney-shaped or like a fan and grows up to 60 cm across with a short lateral stalk anchoring it to the wood. The upper surface is characteristically scaly and the scales are brown and rather feathery in appearance on a yellow background. On the underside the surface is made up of small creamy-coloured pores which connect to tubes supporting the spore-bearing layer. The flesh is thick and succulent when the fungus is in its prime condition, though the whole thing later dries out to become tough and whitish and is then unsuitable for cookery.
■ **Cookery** In the kitchen, *P. squamosus* dries and stores well, retaining its flavour and aroma. It is also one of those species which, from time to time, the more extrovert French chef will flambé in Calvados and serve up as a novelty dish between courses.

Pseudocraterellus sinuosus

■ **Where and when** Sharp eyes are needed to spot this fungus because it is remarkably well camouflaged with the surrounding leaf litter. However, once discovered, there is usually a good amount of it to pick. The fruiting bodies emerge through the soil of deciduous woods in clusters and, at close quarters, look like miniature *Craterellus cornucopioides*. The fungus can be found throughout the autumn but is infrequent, perhaps often overlooked.

■ **Appearance** The cap extends to a maximum of 5 cm across, although it is usually smaller, and is funnel-shaped with a wavy, lobed rim. The colour is generally greyish with tints of cream and brown and it is quite tough and fibrous. Like its larger relative, *Pseudocraterellus* has no true gills on the under surface of the cap but an irregular series of wrinkles which are covered by the spore-bearing layer and which are typically of a pallid creamy colour which becomes more greyish as it merges into the stalk. The fungus has a faintly fruity aroma.

■ **Cookery** *Pseudocraterellus* is moderately recommended for the table having earned some of the excellent properties of the chanterelles. Continental recipe books tend to ignore it, probably on the grounds that it is too small and too difficult to find.

Sparassis crispa

Cauliflower Fungus

■ **Where and when** *Sparassis* emerges from late summer and through most of the autumn but don't expect to find many decent specimens after the end of October. It is by no means common and it grows in coniferous woods typically at the base of pine trees and stumps.

■ **Appearance** This is a dramatic-looking species whose fruiting body consists of a spherical or plump rounded cushion made up of numerous thinly lobed branches spreading from a short stalk rooted in the ground. It can grow to up to 50 cm across. The whole thing looks remarkably like a cauliflower. The overall colour of a fresh specimen is a delicate cream but older specimens turn progressively darker, verging towards dirty tan. The fungus smells sweetish and has a mild taste and, when in the right condition for eating, it should have an evenly pale colour and a crisp feel.

■ **Cookery** Once seen, never forgotten, one of the delights of this fungus for the would-be gourmet is that it is quite impossible to confuse with any other species. It is strictly a 'one-off'. If it possesses any faults, the worst of them is that it tends to get tangled up with pine needles as it grows and ends up looking somewhat like an anaemic porcupine. To collect a fully developed specimen requires, incidentally, a fairly large basket! It should be cut off cleanly at the base, as a complete growth, and as many as possible of the pine needles extracted.

Because of the size, unless one is considering a large dinner party, it will last you for several days. So how does one keep it fresh? The best solution is to immerse the cut stalk in a bowl of water and leave it in the fridge or somewhere cool. It can also be cut into *small* pieces (essential if it is not to rot) and dried or pickled.

Using the fresh material, many people advocate cutting the fruiting body into slices and slowly frying with a little seasoning. The result is mouth-watering if the cooking is done gently and for about 4 minutes. The flavour is mild with slightly nutty tones. On the Continent one of the most popular traditional recipes is to coat the slices with beaten egg before dropping them into the pan.

Surprisingly, in many respects, *Sparassis* gets a generally muted reception from the French. It is merely another species to throw into a mushroom fricassee because of its unusual texture and shape.

Amanita excelsa

(Amanita spissa)

A small number of the *Amanita* species are edible and may be encountered in cookery books, particularly if these have been published in Continental Europe. I have eaten a number of species, including *A. rubescens*, the Blusher, and *A. caesarea*, Caesar's Mushroom, and I can promise that they are excellent. All should be treated with great caution, however, both in the identification and the consumption because they may be confused with closely related species that produce deadly poisons in their tissues. If you decide to experiment with edible *Amanita* species, then it is essential that the whole specimen is taken for examination as some important features are to be found on the extreme base of the stalk.

■ **Where and when** *Amanita excelsa* grows on soil in both deciduous and coniferous woods and is not infrequent in late summer and early autumn.

■ **Appearance** This species has a typical 'mushroom' shape, with patches on the cap and a ring on the stalk. The stalk also swells into a bulbous base. These are all features that typify the *Amanita* genus.

The cap extends to between 6 and 10 cm across and is firm and fleshy. It is greyish or brownish-coloured on its upper surface and has a covering of pallid greyish patches looking rather like hoar frost. These patches are the remnants of the veil or volva that protected the young specimen as it pushed up through the soil. The gills beneath the cap are white, crowded and free (in other words they are not attached directly to the top of the stalk). The cap is supported on a stalk, also white, which extends up to 12 cm in height and is solidly fleshy with little concentric scales appearing on the surface of the lower half. Typically it is deeply embedded in the soil. The white ring, remnant of a secondary, or partial veil, is large though not particularly lax or pendulous.

A chemical test applying sulphuric acid to the cut flesh turns it purple. There is no particular aroma. The most likely confusion arises with the poisonous, but uncommon, *A. pantherina* whose veil patches are pure white, not grey and which has a distinctive ridge at the junction of the stem and swollen base.

■ **Cookery** Tasting moderately mushroomy but otherwise with little to say for itself, *A. excelsa* is probably one of those species for the intrepid fungal gourmet rather than the casual weekend collector.

Amanita rubescens

The Blusher

The same cautionary note must be made here as with *A. excelsa*. The *Amanita* genus includes a number of intensely poisonous species, some deadly. Thus all members must be treated with great caution both in collecting and cooking. Having reiterated the necessary caveat I should also say that I have cooked and eaten *A. rubescens* on several occasions and enjoyed the experience greatly with no ill-effects.

■ **Where and when** The species is very common, growing on soil in both coniferous and broad-leaved woodlands.

■ **Appearance** *Amanita rubescens* displays the typical features of the genus, namely patches on the cap (the remains of the protective volva or veil), a ring on the stalk and a bulbous base. It also has another distinctive characteristic which separates it from others in the genus: it invariably turns reddish when cut or bruised, hence its popular name.

The cap is generally a dull reddish brown, convex or bun-shaped at first and then flattening and extending to 15 cm in diameter. The patches which cover it are pallid red colour but it is important to remember that they can be washed off by rain. On the underside of the cap, the gills are white, or spotted dull reddish, and free from the stalk. The stalk itself is tall and solidly constructed growing up to 14 cm in height and is of a similar colour to the cap. The ring is typically pallid and pendulous. The lower part of the stalk can sometimes be patterned quite strikingly with patches of the volva, and the bulbous base is not generally marked by a distinct ridge. The taste and smell are not distinctive.

■ **Cookery** This is amongst the best of the edible *Amanita* species. Most Continental guides recommend it with a moderate 'gourmet rating' of two stars either as a vegetable in its own right or as an accompaniment to meat dishes.

The fungus should never be eaten raw; it must always be cooked first by simmering and the cooking water discarded. There is nothing particularly alarming about this: one does it regularly with such foods as red kidney beans. Once cooked you may find it quite a delicacy depending on personal taste. The flavour is slightly tart but the piquancy imparts a pleasant tang to the bland flavour of some other fungi. One of the more flamboyant entrepreneurial Victorian mushroom aficionados, the Reverend Worthington G. Smith, described it as 'delicious and perfectly wholesome'. He added that he had not only eaten it himself but had known it to be eaten by many other people. He lived, I believe, to a ripe old age!

Armillaria mellea

(Clitocybe mellea)

Honey Fungus

■ **Where and when** One of the commonest woodland agarics, *Armillaria* appears in dense clumps on deciduous and coniferous stumps. Sometimes it may seem to be growing on soil in proximity to the trunks of living trees, particularly beech but, in fact, the relationship with the tree, living or dead, is always an intimate one and if the fruiting bodies are not emerging directly from the wood they will still be connected with the roots. The fungus is a virulent and destructive parasite spreading over long distances by means of black 'bootlace' mycelial cords which penetrate into, and eventually kill, their host.

Armillaria is a large fleshy fungus appearing throughout the summer and autumn and several sub-species have now been distinguished which separate tall slender forms from squat and bulky ones. Since, however, all of these are edible and good, the fine distinctions are of academic interest.

■ **Appearance** The caps can vary from 4 to 15 cm across, at first convex and then flattened, wavy and sometimes depressed at the centre. In most sub-species, but not all, the stalk bears a ring. The fruiting bodies vary in both shape and colour, which ranges from ochre yellow to tan and even dark brown. As a rule they are palest when immature and darken with age but the cap is always decorated with darkish brown fibrous scales, particularly towards the centre. The gills are white at first becoming tan-coloured and finally darker and spotted with brown. The stalk is thick, tough and fibrous and, like the cap, it is pallid when young becoming similar in colour to the cap as the specimen ages. In older clumps the off-white spores produce a characteristic dusting of caps lower down in the cluster.

■ **Cookery** The fungus is easily recognizable with a bit of practice despite some variation in the general appearance and it is delicious to eat although not to everyone's personal taste. Inexplicably, some

of the French guides to edible mushrooms give it a very low rating, and I have probably seen it on sale more frequently in Italy. Certainly the flavour is strong and *Armillaria* is perhaps best mixed with other fungi of a more bland nature. It is one of my favourites, certainly for nostalgic reasons, because it was one of the first I ever tasted and I have occasionally initiated would-be fungus gourmets by frying up a bunch of fresh caps in an old skillet on a primus stove! Picking bits of sizzling fungi that were growing five minutes earlier out of the pan and sampling them with cold (and probably grubby) fingers on the edge of an autumn woodland has to be one of the gastronomic experiences of a lifetime!

Browsing through the offerings of the old Victorian mycologists, for whose entrepreneurial spirit we have much to be grateful, one comes across C. D. Badham's *Esculent Funguses of England* in which he asserts that this mushroom is 'nauseous and disagreeable however cooked'. Much as one admires the gastronomic stamina of such authors for experimenting with fungi quite so heroically, there is a suspicion that Mr Badham never got past the stage of sniffing the raw specimens of Honey Fungus. Some people do find the mushroom too rich but, having made a regular sortie to the woods at the beginning of each season to collect it for the pan, I still view the prospect with pleasurable anticipation twenty years on from my initiation and I have never suffered ill-effects.

Notwithstanding possible French reservations, the mushroom is much sought after in Continental Europe. Because it is quite strongly flavoured it is often dried, powdered and used as a condiment. My personal preference is to sauté pieces of the fresh young caps in butter with a little chopped shallot. There is an initial acid aroma but this disappears almost at once. The flavour when cooked in this way is hot and almost spicy.

The mushroom, chopped small and marinaded in a little lemon juice, olive oil and seasoning, is also an excellent choice as the dominant flavouring of a rich sauce. This is prepared with chopped onion browned in butter, a little flour to thicken, marjoram, and white wine, and served with a stuffed pasta such as ravioli.

Clitocybe fragrans

This is an inconspicuous little agaric which is perhaps best left alone until you are confident about identification. The species is quite wholesome, with a delightful aroma as its name suggests, and it may appear in Continental guides to edible fungi. The real danger is in confusing *C. fragrans* with some less pleasant members of the group including *C. dealbata* and *C. rivulosa*, both of which grow to a similar size and may be of similar colour but which are deadly poisonous.

■ **Where and when** *Clitocybe fragrans* is a species which appears under deciduous trees, often in moss or thin grass, from late autumn until the early frosts kill off its fruiting bodies but it is not particularly common.

■ **Appearance** The cap measures up to 4 cm across when mature and is flattish or slightly depressed in the centre. It is also hygrophanous, which means that it will readily take up water. Under these circumstances the appearance can alter markedly. Thus when dry it is generally cream-coloured, with a slightly darker centre, but a yellowish tan in damp or wet conditions. The edge of the cap may be finely striated or furrowed. The cap sits on top of a tallish slender stalk, up to 6 cm long, which is of similar colour and to which the gills are joined often running slightly down the stalk (decurrent). The spores are white. The best identification feature is the smell which is unmistakably of aniseed.

■ **Cookery** Because of its distinctive aroma, *C. fragrans* is perhaps best used in omelettes. It is too insubstantial to serve as an independent vegetable.

Clitocybe geotropa

(Clitocybe maxima)

■ **Where and when** One of the largest and most easily recognized members of the *Clitocybe* genus, *C. geotropa* is an excellent addition to anyone's list of fungi for the pot. Occasional rather than frequent in occurrence, it is found in rings or lines on woodland floors where it prefers open habitats on the edges of trees or in grassy clearings.

■ **Appearance** The fruiting body is a fine flesh colour, though often with tinges of buff when young. It stands up to 15 cm tall on a robust and very upright stalk which may be rather swollen at the base, and the cap extends to a meaty and impressive 20 cm across. The combination of size and colour makes *C. geotropa* very easy to spot. At first the cap is convex with a distinct central boss or umbo but as it matures it becomes shallowly funnel-shaped. Take a close look at the edge of the cap because typically it remains incurved. On the underside the gills, of similar colour to the cap, are joined to and run down the stalk (decurrent). The spores are white. There is no distinctive smell other than a pleasant and sweetish 'mushroom' aroma.

■ **Cookery** The taste is delicious and two or three specimens of *C. geotropa* will make a good meal. As always, check that the flesh is free from maggots. It is also an excellent addition to meat dishes.

Clitocybe nebularis

Clouded Agaric

■ **Where and when** Found on soil in woods generally, but particularly under conifers, this mushroom is large and fleshy and often occurs in large groups or rings. It is very common during the autumn months.

■ **Appearance** The cap is at first bun-shaped becoming convex, flattened, and finally a little depressed at the centre with the margin remaining more or less inrolled. It expands up to 20 cm across. The surface is grey, often with a whitish bloom, tinged with buff and darker at the centre. Older specimens tend to be more pallid. The stalk is pallid greyish buff with a slightly swollen base. The flesh is white, thick, easily broken, and fibrous in the stalk. The gills are off-white, decurrent (running down the stalk) and crowded together. The spores are cream-coloured. The smell is strongly of fungus and the taste is sweetish.

■ **Cookery** For some people *C. nebularis* is too strong for eating and it has been known to cause tummy upsets (nothing more serious!). At one time it was called the New Cheese Agaric because the aroma is supposedly reminiscent of cottage cheese. The flavour is, if anything, strongly aromatic when cooked and in Continental Europe it tends to be incorporated with other, more bland-tasting fungi, rather than used as a dish on its own. It is important, as is generally stressed, to pick only young fresh-looking caps, as the species is popular on the dinner menu of slugs, snails and beetles.

Clitocybe odora

(Clitocybe viridis)

Aniseed Agaric

Like *C. fragrans*, this species possesses a delightful aroma of aniseed. Unlike its cousin, the blue-green colour of *C. odora* makes its easily recognizable.

■ **Where and when** This is a medium-sized agaric which emerges from leaf litter, often under beeches but also under other deciduous trees, from late summer until the first frosts of winter. Although some authors describe it as frequent, my own experience of *C. odora* is of more occasional sightings. Perhaps it is just that others have got there first.

■ **Appearance** The cap is convex with a low central hump or umbo in young specimens, but it becomes flattened and rather wavy at the edges as it matures. It can extend up to 8 cm across though usually smaller. The gills run slightly down the stem (decurrent) and are off-white or tinged with the blue-green cap colour. They produce white spores. The stalk is quite short and stocky and is tinged, again, with the cap colour. At the base it is covered with white 'fur'. Try tasting a bit by chewing it on the tip of your tongue. It doesn't just smell of aniseed!

■ **Cookery** As with *C. nebularis* the taste is strong and this fungus is perhaps better suited to use as a flavouring rather than as a meal in its own right. It goes well as a raw ingredient in salads where the pretty colour is an advantage. In Continental Europe it is also sugared to make an improbable glacé fruit sweet, largely because of the attractive colour of the caps.

Clitocybe vibecina

■ **Where and when** Another of the fairly modest edible *Clitocybe* species but one which may often turn up in reasonable numbers during the autumn months. Generally it appears in coniferous woods or on heaths but it is not uncommon in mixed woods. Keep a look-out for it, particularly if you happen to be walking through bracken.

■ **Appearance** The colour of the cap, which is hygrophanous (readily takes up water), ranges from cream when dry to a pale grey-brown in damp conditions and the margin is faintly striated. The cap is faintly convex when young but soon becomes flattened, with a slight depression at the centre, and it extends to a maximum diameter of 5 cm. The gills, which are more or less cap-coloured and produce white spores, run down the stalk (decurrent) which is quite tall (up to 5 cm) and slender. The fruiting body is said to smell and taste mealy but such distinctions are not always as obvious as the guidebooks make out.

■ **Cookery** The species will serve as a vegetable in its own right but is, frankly, unremarkable. It is thin-fleshed and you need to find a reasonable number of specimens to make any kind of a worthwhile meal.

Flammulina velutipes

Velvet Shank

■ **Where and when** This beautiful medium-sized agaric, which always grows on dead or dying wood, is unmistakable in appearance because of the brilliant tan colour of the cap in combination with a stalk which, in its lower half, is a dark and densely velvet brown. *Flammulina velutipes* is one of the limited number of agaric species capable of withstanding frost and therefore it makes its appearance from late autumn right through the winter months to the spring. Since it particularly favours elm as a host, it used to be much more common before the advent of Dutch elm disease. It is still reasonably frequent in occurrence though on other dead deciduous trees, logs and stumps where it grows in clusters.

■ **Appearance** The cap is bright tan at the margin verging to darker tan nearer the centre and is slimy or viscid. In young specimens it is convex but soon becomes flattened and slightly wavy, extending to 10 cm across. The stalk is tough and cartilaginous, cap-coloured only at the top. The flesh is generally thin. The gills are pale yellow with white spores. The taste and smell of the fresh specimens are pleasant but not distinctive.

■ **Cookery** When cooked, the flavour of *F. velutipes* is noticeably piquant and the stems are tough. For this reason it is perhaps best employed as a condiment. The mushrooms can be strung on cotton and hung up to dry then chopped or put through a blender before storage.

Hygrocybe nivea

(Camarophyllus virgineus)

Snowy Wax Cap

■ **Where and when** This is a small species but is common and often appears in considerable numbers. It occurs during the autumn months in short grass on fire breaks, at the edges of woodlands, on roadside verges and, less frequently, in pastures.

■ **Appearance** The cap is white, at first convex or domed, becoming irregularly flattened, and finally depressed at the centre, expanding to 3 cm across. In older specimens the colour may vary towards ivory. As in all members of the *Hygrocybe* genus, the surface of the cap feels greasy or waxy when dry and somewhat slimy in wet weather. The stalk is white, slender, and it typically tapers towards the base. The flesh is white, relatively thick at the centre of the cap, and has no distinctive taste or smell. The gills are decurrent, running down the stalk, white and fairly well spaced from each other. Like the cap they have a waxy feel. The spores are white.

■ **Cookery** Because of its small size, the species is only of limited value in the kitchen. It has, nonetheless, a good reputation as an edible fungus and most Continental European guides give it a moderate two-star rating in terms of a vegetable or as an ingredient in omelettes. Because of its pretty colour it is also useful as a garnish.

Laccaria laccata

The Deceiver

Don't be put off by the name. This agaric emerges in what may seem a confusing variety of appearances but sooner or later, no matter what disguise it tries on, you will develop a 'nose' to recognize it.

■ **Where and when** It is amongst the commonest of all higher fungi and frequently appears on woodland floors in considerable numbers from summer until the first frosts cut it back.

■ **Appearance** The fungus develops a medium-sized fruiting body and the overall colour is brownish, though this ranges from tawny to brick and the gills usually have a pinkish appearance. Older specimens are more dull brown. By and large the cap, gills and stalk are more or less uniform in colour. The cap first appears domed or convex and then becomes flattened with a slightly undulating margin which typically bears fine striations. The surface may have a faintly scurfy appearance. The gills, which are joined to the stalk, produce white spores which often give them a dusty appearance when mature. The stalk is tough, fibrous, often distorted and is generally unevenly flattened in section. There is no obvious smell.

■ **Cookery** Despite its tricky character, one is unlikely to confuse *L. laccata* with anything dangerous. Not the most inspiring of mushrooms with its thin caps and uninteresting colour, its chief benefit lies in that it is extremely common. *Laccaria laccata* is employed mainly in omelettes and as a garnish though it is useful with both meat and fish dishes.

Laccaria amethystea

(Laccaria laccata var. *amethystina)*

Amethyst Agaric

■ **Where and when** When dressed in its real colour, a deep lilac or amethyst, *L. amethystea* is one of the prettiest of all woodland fungi. The conditions have to be damp, though, for the marvellously rich shading to emerge and disappointingly one comes across the fruiting bodies too often when they are partly dried out and the colour has become an insipid pale buff with only a hint of its true beauty.

In some years *L. amethystea* can be extremely common, almost rivalling *L. laccata* in profusion and it may appear in either deciduous or coniferous woods. It is particularly common in beechwoods and I have walked under October beech canopies where, literally, acres have been carpeted with these fungi.

■ **Appearance** The fruiting bodies are of similar size to *L. laccata*, the caps starting off domed or convex and then flattening, sometimes with a slight central depression, and extending up to 6 cm across. The surface also becomes slightly scurfy with age. The stalk is of similar colour to the cap though mealy near the top and it extends into a lilac-coloured mycelium running beneath the surface of the leaf litter. The gills are also lilac and may appear quite widely spaced or distant from each other. The spores are white and may give the gills a dusty appearance when mature. There is no obvious taste or smell.

■ **Cookery** The brilliant colour of this little mushroom makes it an obvious favourite with the artistic chef. Most Continental cookery guides give it the three-star accolade as a colouring garnish and as an addition to omelettes, meat and fish dishes.

Lactarius camphoratus

Curry-scented Milk Cap

■ **Where and when** Emerging predominantly under conifers, these fungi also appear less frequently in deciduous woods, but the ideal place to search them out is a spruce plantation any time from summer to late autumn. I have often walked through forests on a warm dry autumn day when the whole area reeked with their delicious aroma.

■ **Appearance** The caps are reddish brown, sometimes with a darker brown centre which may also have a small central boss, or umbo. The cap emerges in a convex or dome shape and then flattens and depresses and, when fully grown, extends to about 5 cm across. The surface texture of *Lactarius* species is often significant in their correct identification. In *L. camphoratus* the cap surface is matt and never sticky or viscid. The stalk is of similar colour to the cap, extending to 5 cm in height and the gills, which run down the stem (decurrent), are of a pale brown colour and closely crowded together. The strong curry aroma may not be obvious in young specimens or in wet weather, but it becomes very noticeable on drying out. Like all *Lactarius* species, *L. camphoratus* produces 'milk' when the flesh is cut. In this case it is rather watery and mild to taste.

■ **Cookery** One of a limited number of small *Lactarius* species that are worthy of collection for the kitchen, *L. camphoratus*, as its common name indicates, smells strongly of curry, particularly when dry. This is definitely a mushroom suitable for drying, powdering and employing as a condiment. The flavour is too pungent otherwise. It is also worth a moderate rating as an ingredient in omelettes or pasta dishes.

Lactarius deliciosus

Saffron Milk Cap

This is a useful fungus for the mushroom gourmet, quite popular in Continental Europe and fairly easy to identify. It would be hard to confuse with dangerous species, a consideration which makes it a useful inclusion on any beginner's list.

■ **Where and when** Always found growing under, or near, pines or spruce, *L. deliciosus* is a large fleshy agaric with distinctive coloration. Unfortunately in Britain the species is only locally common in England, but it is much more plentiful in Scotland.

■ **Appearance** The caps are domed or convex when they emerge but soon become funnel-shaped with a shallow depression, the margin often remaining incurved for some time. The texture may be slightly sticky. The caps can extend to 10 cm across when mature and are thick and fleshy with a solid feel. The background colour is pale pinkish buff covered with salmony blotches arranged in concentric rings. Sometimes greenish tinges, but never spots, may also be discernible. The stalk is similar in background colour to the cap and develops more distinct salmony blotches which may be in shallow pits. Like the cap, the stalk may have greenish tinges, particularly in older specimens, and is short and stocky, extending to no more than 6 cm in height, frequently less. The gills run slightly down the stalk and are a fleshy pinkish buff colour, becoming more orange or carroty and also tingeing greenish where bruised or otherwise damaged. The spores are pale ochre when massed together on a white paper. As in all members of the *Lactarius* genus, the flesh oozes 'milk' when cut. In *L. deliciosus* it is a dark orange or carrot colour slowly fading to greyish green on exposure to the air. The taste of the milk is slightly bitter. Only one other species is likely to be confused with this one: *L. deterrimus*, which grows in similar habitats; it is also safe to eat, though not quite as palatable, and it differs mainly in the colour of the cut flesh which becomes purplish after about half an hour of exposure. The cap and stalk are also likely to develop more obvious greenish spots.

■ **Cookery** In his book *Esculent Funguses of England*, the Victorian mycophile C. D. Badham remarks that this mushroom was exhibited for sale in prodigious quantities in the open markets of Marseilles about a hundred years ago and describes it as being 'very luscious eating, full of rich gravy with a little of the flavour of mussels'. I have a sneaky feeling that Mr Badham may have had shellfish from that Marseilles market in his shopping bag too! Badham suggests baking the caps in a pie dish, with seasoning and a piece of butter on each, for 45 minutes and then covering with a white sauce prepared from the juices. There is a slight tendency for the bitterness to come through if the mushrooms are merely sautéed.

Lactarius deliciosus qualifies gallantly as an ingredient of ketchup or chutney and it is a suitable candidate for drying.

Lactarius glyciosmus

Coconut-scented Milk Cap

■ **Where and when** Another of the smaller edible *Lactarius* members with a very distinctive character, *L. glyciosmus* smells unmistakably of coconuts! It is common and found growing particularly under birch trees but it will also appear with other broad-leaved trees. It occurs throughout the late summer and autumn until the first frosts.

■ **Appearance** The cap, buff with a greyish or lilac tinge, is domed or convex when immature, later expanding to 5 cm across and becoming slightly depressed at the centre. The stalk is of similar but paler colour and, though stocky in appearance, is easily broken. Inside it may be partially hollow or filled with a soft 'pith'. The gills are pale yellow or flesh-coloured, crowded together and running a little way down the stalk (decurrent). They produce creamy white spores. When the flesh is cut, as in all *Lactarius* species, it produces a 'milk'. Try a little on the tip of your tongue. It will taste mild at first but then rather hot and acrid.

■ **Cookery** With its interesting aroma, this species is best suited to use in omelettes and pasta dishes. Not to be recommended raw.

Lactarius blennius

Slimy Milk Cap

■ **Where and when** This is a largish *Lactarius* species which appears during the autumn months. *L. blennius* is very common in broad leaved woods generally.

■ **Appearance** The cap colour is pale olive to greenish grey with darker, more or less concentric bands of blotches. It expands up to 10 cm across, at first domed and then flattened or depressed at the centre. The surface is sticky when dry and viscid when moist, and the flesh is whitish and fairly solid. The stalk is paler than the cap and the flesh is whitish. The gills are whitish when young, turning more buff with age and running slightly down the stem (decurrent). They generate cream-coloured spores. The milk, typical of the *Lactarius* group, is hot and acrid.

■ **Cookery** Although *L. blennius* may have a rather off-putting slimy feel in damp weather, the texture changes on cooking. The culinary value is unexceptional and the species provokes little interest in Continental Europe but it is worth experimenting with.

Lactarius subdulcis

■ **Where and when** This is a very comon small to medium *Lactarius* species which makes a pleasant meal if you can manage to collect a reasonable quantity. It is most likely to appear with beech trees but can be found in any broad-leaved woods and the fruiting bodies emerge from late summer until early winter. Not the easiest of species for a beginner to identify and you may be advised to have it pointed out by an expert and become familiar with its appearance.

■ **Appearance** The cap is reddish brown to cinnamon-coloured (in common with several other similarly sized *Lactarius* species), domed or convex at first but expanding up to 7 cm across and shallowly depressed with a little boss or umbo at the centre. The surface is smooth and matt and the flesh is rather thin. The stalk is of similar colour and texture to the cap though often paler in its upper half. The gills are either very slightly extended down the stalk (weakly decurrent) or simply attached to it (adnate). They are pallid buff in colour and the spores are cream. Try the milk which is produced from the cut flesh on the tip of your tongue. It should be mild at first and then slightly bitter. As an additional test, dab a drop of it on a white handkerchief. In some similar-looking species the milk will turn yellow, but that of *L. subdulcis* remains white.

■ **Cookery** Like most of the *Lactarius* family, this species is poorly rated by Continental cooks.

Lepiota procera

Field Parasol

If there is any danger with the *Lepiota* genus, it lies in possible confusion with the dangerously poisonous *Amanita* species. Providing, however, one observes the criteria sensibly (the essential differences between the two genera are described fully in the opening chapter), the large parasol mushrooms can be collected and enjoyed with confidence.

■ **Where and when** One of the biggest of all agarics, *L. procera* is also one of the gourmet treats amongst wild mushrooms but it is unfortunately less than common. Generally the fruiting bodies make their appearance in pastures and on the grassy edges of woodlands and they emerge from mid-summer until early autumn.

■ **Appearance** The caps sit on tall, elegant stalks and expand to 25 cm in the largest specimens. At first the cap is egg-shaped or ovate but then it expands more or less flat apart from a central boss or umbo. The background is a pallid greyish brown which breaks up into darker coarse scales that give the cap a shaggy appearance. Though it is fleshy it also has a soft, flabby feel. The stalk is tall, up to 30 cm in height, tough and fibrous, and covered with a brownish-grey felty outer surface. As the stalk expands lengthwise, the surface breaks up into belted markings and reveals a white under surface. In the upper third is a large, movable two-tiered ring, white on the upper side, grey-brown below, and at the base of the stalk is an off-centre bulb. The young cap can be easily twisted off the stalk.

The gills are white and free from the stalk with a narrow channel separating them. They produce white spores. The smell is slightly mushroomy and the flesh has a distinctly sweet taste.

■ **Cookery** *Lepiota procera* stands up magnificently both cooked and raw. It is an excellent ingredient in sauces and goes particularly well with meat dishes. Not to be recommended for use with omelettes and pastas though. It is too chunky.

When preparing any of the large *Lepiota* species for the pan, throw away the stalks. They are too tough to be of culinary use. The scales are edible and add an attractive feature to the vegetable.

Immature caps make excellent receptacles for whatever filling takes your fancy! There are a number of excellent recipes to be found. Onion, Gruyère cheese and breadcrumbs with a liberal addition of herbs and seasoning is one of my favourites, but you may prefer to enjoy the caps chopped and sautéed in a little butter.

Try braising a pair of fully expanded caps for 20 minutes in a shallow baking dish with butter and seasoning. Grill some good honey-smoked back bacon and toast three slices of bread. Drain the caps, assemble all the ingredients, and you have the finest of toasted 'brunch' sandwiches.

Lepiota rhacodes

Shaggy Parasol

■ **Where and when** *Lepiota rhacodes* is a large handsome and fleshy mushroom, instantly recognizable. It is fairly common and appears right through the summer and autumn in woodlands and shrubberies, particularly in the vicinity of conifers. It rarely emerges as a solitary specimen and there is often a group of half a dozen or more in close proximity to one another.

■ **Appearance** When the fruiting body first emerges the unopened cap is egg-shaped or ovate, but as the mushroom matures it expands more or less flat, other than for a low hump or umbo at the centre, to 15 cm across, making it one of the largest of any fruiting bodies, though still small by comparison with the Field Parasol (*L. procera*). The surface of the cap is brownish but breaks up into large coarse scales which tend to be darker brown, particularly at the edges, and which reveal a pallid under surface giving the cap a strikingly shaggy appearance. The cap rests on a tall stalk up to 15 cm in height which is tough and fibrous in consistency. It swells into a basal bulb which is usually displaced to one side and it should have no evidence of a volval bag attached to it. The stalk is pallid but bruises a dirty reddish-brown colour and bears a prominent two-tiered ring in the upper third, usually movable on the stalk. It is also generally easy to twist the cap off the stalk. The gills are white but bruise reddish; they bear white spores. The gills are free in *Lepiota* species and two should be separated by a narrow channel. The whole mushroom smells pleasantly aromatic.

■ **Cookery** Fruiting bodies may persist for a long time, particularly in fairly dry summer conditions and it is important to pick them when young and fresh. Look out for worm tunnels or signs of discoloration.

Lepiota rhacodes is a delicious species. In some allergic individuals, it can cause stomach upset but *L. rhacodes* is not poisonous in any conventional sense and this sort of individual reaction can technically occur with almost any mushroom.

Essentially the same methods of cookery that apply to *L. procera* can be employed and this species is considered to possess a similar value as a vegetable but is perhaps thought rather less versatile as an addition to other dishes.

Lepiota rhacodes var. *hortensis*

■ **Where and when** This palatable mushroom, and third member of a 'trio' of large parasols, is subtly distinct from *L. rhacodes* in both appearance and occurrence. As its name suggests, the *hortensis* variety generally appears on rich, compost-fed soil in gardens rather than in woodlands.

■ **Appearance** The two fungi bear caps of similar size but in the garden variety, apart from the central boss, which is of a uniform colour, the outer surface of the cap breaks up into large angular scales which are distinctly reddish brown whilst the layer exposed beneath is white. The stalk is much shorter than in *L. rhacodes* but bears the same loosely fitted double ring and also ends in an off-centre bulb. The stalk is white but turns a dull brown where bruised. The gills are also white, bruising brownish, and they are free from the stalk. The cut flesh turns a red colour through less dramatically than in *L. rhacodes* and the taste is mushroomy with a pleasant though not so strongly aromatic aroma. Both varieties emerge at the same time of year.

■ **Cookery** Probably the weakest of the trio in terms of flavour and texture, var. *hortensis* is well worth trying nevertheless.

Lepiota excoriata

Although this medium to large *Lepiota* is edible and good to eat, it could be confused with some less palatable individuals and it is therefore advisable to have it identified by an expert until one is really confident about its appearance. There are, unfortunately, a few dangerously poisonous all-white species of fungi. Check the distinctions between *Amanita* and *Lepiota* fungi described on page 22.

■ **Where and when** Don't search for this one in woods: it is strictly an inhabitant of late summer and autumn pastureland (which actually eliminates most of the villains). The specimens in the illustration are typical of some which grow prolifically on water-meadows near Glastonbury in my home county of Somerset.

■ **Appearance** The cap is white with tiny pallid buff scales, and is egg-shaped or ovoid when it first pushes through the grass but then quickly expands into a flatly domed profile. The biggest caps extend to 10 cm across. Each is carried on a stalk which is also white, smooth and ending at the base in a slight thickening rather than a distinct bulb. As in most *Lepiota* species, there is an obvious ring, white but quite narrow and difficult to move. The gills and spores are a very pale cream or off-white and the gills are separate, or free, from the top of the stalk. It is usually quite easy to twist the cap off the stalk. The specimens have no obvious aroma.

■ **Cookery** In Continental European guides, *L. excoriata* earns a three-star rating as a vegetable and when employed with meat dishes.

Marasmius oreades

Fairy Ring Champignon

This species is one of the best known of all wild mushrooms and is much valued in Continental Europe where it is often dried and used as flavouring for soups and casseroles.

■ **Where and when** Essentially a species of lawns and pastureland, the smallish fruiting bodies grow in the distinctive, ever-broadening rings that are so often an ingredient of fairy tales. They appear throughout the summer and autumn months and can even emerge in a mild winter. Like the other members of the *Marasmius* genus, the fruiting bodies can shrivel into tough, leathery lumps but will revive in damp conditions.

■ **Appearance** The cap is a tan colour when moist but dries much paler to cream or buff. Extending up to 5 cm across, it is convex at first and then more or less flattened with a large central boss or umbo. The margin often appears grooved or wrinkled. Feel the flesh of this specimen; despite its small size, in the centre of the cap it is quite firm and 'meaty'. The cap sits on a stalk which is of similar buff colour though generally more pallid. It is quite tough and may penetrate a little way into the soil like a small root. The gills are pallid at first and then buff-coloured. They become more or less widely separated as the cap matures, alternating with shorter intermediates, and they produce white spores. The species is said to smell of sawdust with almondy undertones.

■ **Cookery** *M. oreades* is equally valuable in sauces and soups, as a vegetable dish, as an addition to meat and fish dishes, or as a flavouring in omelettes and pasta dishes. It also provides a first-class condiment. Care must be taken when collecting not to confuse it with some dangerously poisonous, and similarly sized *Clitocybe* species, *C, rivulosa* and *C. dealbata*. The latter, in particular, grows in similar locations and at the same time of year but it is buff with a dusty white tone, never properly tan-coloured, and slightly depressed at the centre. The gills are crowded and usually more or less decurrent (running down the stalk). It does not 'root'.

Marasmius oreades is strongly flavoured and it dries and stores extremely well. The fungi can be collected, sorted, separated from their stalks which tend to be overly tough, and threaded on long pieces of cotton before hanging across the kitchen to dry.

The traditional use in England has been as a flavouring in soups and steak and kidney pie. One of the more die-hard Victorian mycophiles, the Reverend Worthington G. Smith, advocates preparing a dish of *M. oreades* in its own right by simply sautéeing in butter which, he states, produces a flavour exquisitely rich and delicious. Given the fact that, on at least one occasion, he admits to having collected the wrong specimens by mistake and been extremely ill for several hours afterwards, his is the praise of a serious aficionado!

Melanoleuca cognata

(Tricholoma cognatum)

This is one of two members of the limited *Melanoleuca* genus which are edible and worth getting to know. These species used to be included in *Tricholoma* and have certain features in common with species of that genus, including large fruiting bodies with broad flattish caps. They were placed in a separate genus because of differences in the microscopic characteristics of their spores. As their name suggests, all are tan, brown or brownish grey.

■ **Where and when** It is not particularly common but look out for *M. cognata* growing on soil in coniferous woodlands chiefly in the autumn. It sometimes appears in the spring but much less frequently.

■ **Appearance** It is almost entirely a dull yellowish tan, sometimes with greyish tints. The cap is shiny and either flattened or very slightly convex up to 10 cm across. It is supported by a stalk which may show faint streaks or striations and which is swollen at the base. The gills and spores are more of a pale ochre yellow colour.

■ **Cookery** I am not wildly enthusiastic about this species. Its taste is moderate and the texture tends to be a little limp.

Mycena haematopus

(Mycena cruenta)

■ **Where and when** This is a not uncommon edible fungus which grows in delicate but striking clumps on old broad-leaved tree stumps throughout the autumn season.

■ **Appearance** The colour of the conical, or bell-shaped, caps varies according to age and weather; the damper the conditions, the darker the shade. In the wet they are dull greyish brown sometimes with a wine tinge and with a striped or striated margin. When they dry out they become pallid and slightly pink. They grow up to 4 cm across. The stalks are long and slender and paler than the caps, often fused together in substantial numbers, and the gills are at first white becoming pinkish as the fruiting bodies mature. The spores are white.

The most distinctive identification feature, suggested by the name *haematopus*, is only revealed when the stalk is broken. It exudes a deep blood-red juice.

■ **Cookery** Most Continental mushroom cookery writers turn their noses up at the *Mycena* species because they lack real substance, or a flavour which would compensate for the absence of flesh. *Mycena haematopus* is probably best employed as a component of a mixed vegetable dish with other, more substantial mushrooms.

Mycena pura

■ **Where and when** This is a common member of the *Mycena* genus which grows singly but often in groups on the floor of beechwoods from summer to winter. (*Note*: the specimens shown here are covered in pine needles from conifers growing near the beeches under which this fungus is found.) It is capable of withstanding a degree or so of frost.

■ **Appearance** The overall colour is a distinctive pink or lilac, becoming paler in dry weather. The caps are variable in size from 2 to 5 cm across, generally either rounded convex, or flattish with a broad central hump or umbo. The pinkish gills are attached to the stalk and produce white spores, and the stalk itself is tall, fairly slender, stiff and tinged with the cap colour.

The easiest identification feature, apart from the colour (there are a limited number of pink fungi), is the smell. Remember to rub part of the fruiting bodies between your fingers to release the odour chemicals. The taste is mild but the aroma is distinctly radishy.

■ **Cookery** In culinary terms the same comments apply to *M. pura* as to *M. haematopus*.

Oudemansiella mucida

(Armillaria mucida)

Porcelain Agaric

This mushroom has a special place in my affections. It is, beyond doubt, one of the most delicate and beautiful of all fungi. Seen in early morning sunshine it possesses a glistening, translucent quality. In the reference books it used to be placed side by side with the Honey fungus *Armillaria mellea*.

■ **Where and when** It grows, as a parasite, on the trunks of living beech trees and you may need to cast your eyes upwards to find it. It is surprisingly common and can appear sprouting from the bark in large clusters high above the ground as well as at lower levels. The fruiting bodies emerge from late summer until about mid-November.

■ **Appearance** The fruiting bodies start life a pale grey but become a pure, semi-translucent white, sometimes with a slight yellowish tinge in the centre of the cap. The most distinctive feature, apart from the colour, is the production of gluten which makes the caps glistening and slimy, often with drops of clear fluid suspended from the edges. The caps can extend to 8 cm across, at first convex then becoming flattened, bearing white gills. The spores are also white. The caps are carried on slender white stalks with small delicate rings above which the stalks may be faintly striated.

■ **Cookery** If you can bear to cut such gloriously beautiful things down, don't let the gluten put you off eating these fungi: it is easily removed by washing. They are best employed as a garnish for cooked meat and fish dishes, or as a vegetable making a stark contrast with dark fungi such as *Craterellus cornucopioides*.

Russula aeruginea

Grass Green Russula

Because of its unusual colour, this is one of the more readily identifiable *Russula* species. Fungi lack chlorophyll in their make-up so very few possess a truly grass-green colour. This, however, as its name implies, is one of the exceptions.

■ **Where and when** Whilst quite frequent in occurrence, *R. aeruginea* is limited to growing in birch copses and woods, often in fairly wet ground.

■ **Appearance** It is a largish, fleshy fungus, sitting low to the ground on a short stout stalk and, like all *Russula* species, its gills have a brittle, waxy feel.

The cap emerges in a bun-shape, and becomes more or less flattened, extending up to 8 cm across. It is smooth, apart from a slight furrowing at the edge and the uniformly green colour may be stained with rust-like spots. Try peeling the cap. The outer 'skin' should come away easily half way towards the centre, but no further, revealing firm white flesh. The stalk is white and smooth and the gills are also white, usually forked and almost free of attachment to the top of the stalk. The spores are cream-coloured.

Nibble a little of the cap on the tip of your tongue. It should be faintly hot after a short while.

■ **Cookery** All the *Russula* species listed here are safe and palatable. Because they generally possess firm flesh and bright cap colours they contribute a pretty and intriguing decoration to fresh salads when sliced thinly and laid over more bland colours of lettuce, cress and avocado. Some *Russula* species readily attract woodland grubs which quickly spoil their appearance. They also tend to become spongy. It is important, therefore, to collect only young, firm, and really fresh-looking material. Have a good sniff at what you pick. It must smell sweetly mushroomy without any hint of the fishy odour which signals that things are past their best.

Russula albonigra

(Russula anthracina)

This is a good edible *Russula* which changes its appearance substantially throughout the life of the fruiting body. This needs to be borne in mind when hunting for it. The Latin name of the species gives the strongest clue and it might well be tagged the 'black and white mushroom'.

■ **Where and when** Though not particularly common, *R. albonigra* produces large and fleshy caps pushing through the surface of the ground during the late summer and autumn months, often in thin grass in shade at the edges of forest rides. They appear under both broad-leaved and coniferous trees.

■ **Appearance** The caps at first are white and flattish bun-shaped but as they mature and expand into broad saucers, up to 12 cm across, they become progressively more blackened or brownish black. The margin tends to remain gently incurved. The surface may be slightly sticky but is otherwise dry and it peels three-quarters of the way to the centre.

The stalk, a little shorter than the cap diameter, changes colour with the cap and the cut flesh also discolours blackish. The gills are a distinctive feature. They are closely crowded together, with shorter ones interspersed and are arc-shaped in profile, running a little down the stalk (decurrent). The spores are white. The taste, when a small piece is nibbled, is mild or slightly bitter.

■ **Cookery** The specimens are only worth collecting for the table when young and more or less white in colour. Once there is any appreciable amount of black present, forget them. There are, incidentally, a number of other whitish-blackish *Russula* species with which *R. albonigra* might be confused. They have varying degrees of flavour, some less palatable than others, but none are poisonous.

Russula atropurpurea

This is one of the commonest of the edible *Russula* species though, as with so many of the genus, it needs to be identified with some care. Many of the more brightly coloured *Russula* species are prone to become washed out and appear more faded than the guidebook illustrations suggest.

■ **Where and when** Generally *R. atropurpurea* is to be found on the ground under oaks and beeches, though it also occurs with conifers.

■ **Appearance** It is a medium-sized fleshy species, the caps extending to 10 cm across, at first bun-shaped and then flattened with a depression at the centre. The colour of the cap is deep reddish purple verging to almost black at the centre. The stalk is white and the gills are similarly coloured or pale cream, shedding off-white spores. The white flesh is at first firm and rather resilient, later becoming softer and more brittle.

A little of the flesh chewed and tasted on the tip of the tongue is mild in old specimens, but hot in younger ones and it has a distinctly fruity aroma, reminiscent of apples.

■ **Cookery** See *R. aerugina*.

Russula claroflava

Yellow Bog Russula

■ **Where and when** This is a pretty and distinctive mushroom. There are a number of *Russula* species with yellow caps but *R. claroflava* is restricted more or less to wet, swampy ground under birch trees. It appears chiefly in the autumn but can also produce fruiting bodies from late spring and through the summer months and it is locally quite common.

■ **Appearance** The caps are medium-sized, extending to 10 cm across, and fairly fleshy. Bun-shaped when young, later becoming more expanded with a small depression at the centre, they are bright yellow or ochre and slightly shiny and sticky when damp. The cap cuticle can be peeled half way and the flesh is white though it bruises a darkish grey. The margin may be slightly grooved in older specimens. The gills are pale ochre and are barely joined to the top of the stalk. The spores are similarly coloured.

■ **Cookery** See *R. aerugina*.

Russula grisea

■ **Where and when** Almost identical to *R. ionochlora* (also edible) in appearance and habitat, this species is really only told apart by microscopic characteristics. Like *R. ionochlora* it is restricted to beechwoods, appearing through the summer and early autumn months. Most of the field guides list *R. grisea* as being uncommon but that is perhaps attributable to the difficulty of telling it apart from some other species.

■ **Appearance** This is small to medium as *Russula* species go, the caps extending only to 7 cm across. They first appear bun-shaped but become irregularly expanded, often with an undulating surface. The cap colour is typically a mixture of muddy greys and browns with faint wine tinges, in itself a feature which leads to the species being overlooked.

The flesh is white, as is the stalk, and the gills are creamy-coloured, almost free from the top of the stalk. The taste of the flesh, chewed and tasted on the tip of the tongue, is generally mild though it can be hot in young specimens.

■ **Cookery** See *R. aerugina*.

Russula lutea

■ **Where and when** This is another small to medium-sized edible *Russula* species with distinctive coloration on the cap. The fruiting bodies can be found quite frequently on the ground under a variety of broad-leaved trees, emerging from late summer to early autumn.

■ **Appearance** The cap is wholly egg yellow sometimes tipped with apricot or pinkish coral. It emerges in a bun-shape and then expands up to 7 cm across and may be depressed at the centre. The flesh is fragile, white, and the cap peels over almost its entire surface. The stalk is white and the gills and spores are deep egg yellow. Try tasting a little of the flesh on the tip of your tongue. It should be very mild. Older specimens have a distinct aroma of apricots.

■ **Cookery** See *R aeruginosa*.

Russula ochroleuca

Common Yellow Russula

■ **Where and when** Probably the commonest of all the *Russula* species, *R. ochroleuca* can sometimes be found in large numbers in an area of woodland. It appears with both broad-leaved and coniferous trees from late summer to the first frosts of winter.
■ **Appearance** It is a largish, fleshy mushroom, the ochre yellow caps extending to 10 cm across. When they first emerge they are bun-shaped but then expand into flattened plates often with a shallow depression at the centre. The ochre colour may sometimes be tinged greenish and the margin becomes faintly grooved in older specimens. The cap cuticle peels across three-quarters of its radius, revealing white flesh. The stalk is white and often rather club-shaped. Gills and spores are pale cream and the gills are joined to the top of the stalk. Taste can be mild or rather hot according to age and there is no obvious smell.
■ **Cookery** See *R aerugina*.

Russula xerampelina

One of a number of large fleshy *Russula* species that possess reddish-coloured caps, *R. xerampelina* can be distinguished by the fishy or lobster-like smell of older specimens and by the colour reaction of the flesh when rubbed with iron salts.

■ **Where and when** The species is common, occurring from late summer to late autumn, and emerging on soil under broad-leaved trees, particularly oak and beech.

■ **Appearance** The cap colour varies but is typically brick red, sometimes darker at the centre, less frequently purplish wine or cinnamon red. It can become washed out and pallid in wet weather. The cap is at first button-like, expanding into a rather lumpy convex bun with a depressed centre, up to 12 cm across. The surface is smooth and dry, though tending to be viscid in wet weather, and the cuticle only peels a short distance towards the centre. In older specimens the margin becomes grooved. The stalk is white but bruises brownish yellow. The flesh is white and fairly solid. The gills are cream-coloured or pale ochre yellow and moderately thick; spore coloration is similar.

If the flesh is rubbed with salts of iron it rapidly turns olive green. The taste is mild and the aroma distinctive.

■ **Cookery** See *R. aerugina*.

Tricholoma cingulatum

■ **Where and when** Usually associated with willow trees, this small to medium-sized *Tricholoma* species makes an appetizing dish if you can find enough specimens growing together. The fruiting bodies emerge, on soil, from late summer to late autumn.

■ **Appearance** The cap is characteristically pale greyish brown or mouse-coloured and covered with felt. It first appears as a button, becoming convex and expanding to 6 cm across. Typically it has a low hump or umbo. The stalk is white, slender, and bears a distinctive woolly ring near the apex. It is worth noting that this is the only member of the *Tricholoma* genus to bear a ring. The flesh is white and possesses a mealy taste and smell. The gills are white, sinuate or notched close to where they join the stem, and produce white spores.

■ **Cookery** Unprepossessing!

Tricholoma gambosum

(Calocybe gambosum)

St George's Mushroom

■ **Where and when** Said, by tradition, to make its appearance on St George's Day, 23 April, this mushroom is a 'must' for any would-be fungus gourmet. The actual dates that the fruiting bodies emerge vary according to the state of the weather but, generally speaking, they reach their optimum size a week or so later. The specimens in the illustration were found and photographed on May Day. *Tricholoma gambosum* is, at best, an occasional find but well worthwhile searching for on roadside verges, in pastures and at the grassy edges of woodlands. In pastures it often occurs in rings.

■ **Appearance** The cap is creamy white becoming more buff with age, button-shaped at first, then convex and finally irregularly expanded up to 15 cm across. The surface is smooth though prone to cracking and the margin tends to remain inrolled. The stalk is similarly coloured, thick and often curved. The flesh is white, solid and brittle. The gills are white, turning more buff with age, very crowded and narrow (revealed when the cap is sliced open), i.e. most of the cap area is taken up with flesh. The spores are white. The taste and smell are distinctly mealy.

■ **Cookery** *T. gambosum* can best be thought of as a spring champignon and as one of the few edible fungi which appear early in the year, it is worth looking out for. It is versatile in its culinary use and it looks, smells and tastes not unlike a field mushroom. Because it has a good firm texture when young it can be used raw as a salad garnish, it sautées well and has a good though quite mild flavour. One aesthetic advantage which you may find useful is the colour. Since the gills do not darken the mature specimen is pure white.

Tricholoma terreum

■ **Where and when** This is a medium-sized *Tricholoma* with obvious distinguishing features, generally found growing under conifers and often in large numbers. The fruiting bodies emerge through the soil from late summer to late autumn.
■ **Appearance** The caps are at first bun-shaped and then expand up to 7 cm across with a slightly undulating profile and a low, broad, central hump or umbo. The cap surface is grey and covered with a distinctive felt whilst the stem is white and has a faintly silky sheen. The gills are white or pale grey with short intermediate members and the spores are also white. There is no distinctive smell and the taste is mushroomy (a species of similar appearance, *T. cingulatum*, tastes distinctly mealy).

Tricholomopsis rutilans

(Tricholoma rutilans)

Plums and Custard

■ **Where and when** This has to be one of the most easily recognized agaric mushrooms in the woods and it is also extremely common through the late summer and autumn months. Look for the species on or around old conifer stumps, often in wiry grass.

■ **Appearance** Plums and Custard is aptly named: the flesh of the cap is pale custard yellow and is covered with fine plum-coloured scales. The stalk is similarly decorated though less densely. This is a good-sized, fleshy agaric, the caps expanding to 12 cm across, wavy, with a low hump or umbo at the centre and a slightly incurved margin. The flesh is pale yellow and the gills are a deep custard yellow, producing white spores. There is no obvious taste and the specimens are said to smell like rotten wood.

■ **Cookery** The credit rating for *T. rutilans* in cookery is open to dispute – some authors enthuse, others do not! In any event it is not poisonous.

Lepista nuda

(Tricholoma nudum; Rhodopaxillus nudus)

Wood Blewit

■ **Where and when** *Lepista nuda* is common in a variety of habitats, from mixed woodlands to hedgerows and even suburban gardens, the fruiting bodies emerging during the autumn months and often making a showing in early winter.

■ **Appearance** This was, at one time, classed with the *Tricholoma* genus, but the *Lepista* species were placed in their own distinct genus because they produce pale pink spores, rather than white or cream. Both genera display a similar overall appearance.

A large, fleshy agaric, the caps emerge in a shallow bun-shape and then expand, up to 12 cm across, becoming wavy in profile and finally depressed into shallow saucers. The surface is smooth, typically pale tan-coloured when damp, drying almost to buff, although the very young caps bear a lilac tinge. Often the cap surface has a polished sheen. The stalk is lilac or bluish lilac, has a fibrous appearance, and may become slightly bulbous at the base. The flesh is similarly coloured and firm. The gills are crowded together and of a rich lilac colour when young though, as the specimens age, they become faded and finally buff-coloured. The spores are pale pink. The mushrooms have a delicious, slightly aromatic smell and a sweetish taste.

■ **Cookery** This is one of the finest of edible mushrooms and, if you turn the cap to see the underside, reassuringly distinctive. Extremely versatile, *L. nuda* was at one time the most popular market mushroom in the Midland shires of England before being ousted by the common white species of *Agaricus* that we purchase today. It stands as a first-class vegetable in its own right but also lends itself well to use as an accompaniment to both meat and fish dishes and to sauces and soups. It can also be sliced raw and incorporated in salads.

Lepista saeva

Field Blewit

■ **Where and when** This is a deliciously edible 'sister' species to *L. nuda* but grows in a distinctly different habitat, restricted to pasture fields and mown grass where the fruiting bodies often appear in rings. It is less common than *L. nuda* but still quite frequent in occurrence and is one of the late showing agarics, emerging from autumn until early winter.

■ **Appearance** *Lepista saeva* is a large fleshy mushroom. The caps are a pale brown, at first bun-shaped then flattened, undulating in profile, and finally somewhat depressed. They extend up to 10 cm across. The stalk is lilac-coloured, fibrous, and the base is typically swollen. The flesh is thick and firm. The gills are crowded together and flesh-coloured. They generate pale pink spores.

Lepista saeva has a tempting aroma and taste not unlike that of *L. nuda* though less strong.

■ **Cookery** In spite of being an excellent mushroom for the pot, the Continental guides to edibility often rate *L. saeva* poorly, which seems unfair to such a tasty specimen. Use it essentially in the same way as *L. nuda*.

Galerina mutabilis

(Pholiota mutabilis)

■ **Where and when** *Galerina mutabilis* is a medium-sized fungus, occurring very commonly, and often in large clusters on stumps or logs of broad-leaved trees. The fruiting bodies appear from spring to the onset of winter frosts.

■ **Appearance** The cap is at first domed or convex, becoming more or less flattened with a low hump or umbo in the centre. It expands to 6 cm across. In wet weather it is a tan or date brown colour when damp. It dries out from the centre to a pale cream or ochre yellow, reminiscent of chamois leather, and frequently appears two-toned. The stalk is of similar colour to the cap with a thin dark brown ring near the apex. The surface is scaly below the ring and more or less smooth above. The flesh is pallid. The gills are at first pallid, becoming date brown as they mature. The spores are deep ochre yellow. The taste and smell are not distinctive.

■ **Cookery** This is a first-rate mushroom for the kitchen. It is just possible to confuse *G. mutabilis* with the Honey Fungus (*Armillaria mellea*). Since the latter is also edible there will be no culinary disaster ensuing if you do get them mixed up, but it is good, nonetheless, to get the two species sorted out. *Galerina mutabilis* is strongly flavoured which makes it an ideal addition to soups and casseroles. It also has the advantage of appearing quite early in the season when few other edible mushrooms are about in the wild.

It is highly rated as a cooked vegetable dish in its own right but is also excellent as an ingredient of soups and when employed as a garnish. It has also been recommended for use in omelettes, with meats, and as an accompaniment to seafood dishes. It is not recommended for use raw in salads but is otherwise a good all-round mushroom.

Paxillus involutus

■ **Where and when** The fruiting bodies are large and fleshy. They are extremely common and appear throughout the late summer and autumn months. The most frequent locations are under birches and on heath, though the fungus is found in most broad-leaved woodlands.

■ **Appearance** The cap is at first domed or convex becoming expanded and funnel-shaped but always retaining an inrolled rim until very old. It extends up to 12 cm across. The cap colour is rusty or hazel brown and downy when dry, otherwise slightly sticky. The stalk is cap-coloured and fleshy. The flesh is creamy in the cap, becoming more brownish in the base of the stalk. The gills are pale cream when young, becoming brown as the spores ripen and they are decurrent, running down the stem, and crowded together. The spores are brown.

■ **Cookery** This species is included less as a culinary suggestion than as a warning. Many Continental guidebooks list it as edible and excellent. Opinions, however, have now changed and it is best avoided. At least one prominent French guide to *'champignons comestibles'* gives *P. involutus* a three-star rating. By contrast, one equally prominent English author describes the same species as poisonous and possibly deadly. I suspect that neither extreme is correct. The current opinion seems to be that certain allergic individuals can react to the fungus if they consume it in quantity over a period of time when it will cause serious stomach upsets. My advice is to err on the side of caution and leave this species to others to sample if they wish to do so.

Agaricus arvensis

(Psalliota arvensis)

Horse Mushroom

■ **Where and when** One of the biggest of the *Agaricus* field mushrooms, this is definitely a species worth getting to know. It is not dissimilar in appearance to the Common Field Mushroom (*A. campestris*), but reaches a substantially larger size and possesses a distinct aroma. Not generally common, it emerges in pastures or amongst scrub and is typically found growing in rings.

■ **Appearance** The large fleshy caps are at first egg-shaped or ovoid but soon begin to expand into shallowly domed plates measuring up to 20 cm across. They are a pale creamy colour and the full-grown specimens are usually visible in a field from some distance away. The stalk is tallish, up to 10 cm in height, of similar colour to the cap, smooth, and bearing a prominent two-tiered ring towards the apex, the lower layer of which splits and is closely applied to the stalk surface. The base of the stalk is often slightly swollen. The flesh is firm in the cap though in the stalk it becomes hollowed and pithy. The young gills are pallid then quickly pink and finally chocolate brown. They are free from the apex of the stalk. The spores are a dark purplish brown. The aroma of several edible *Agaricus* species, including this one, is strongly reminiscent of aniseed.

■ **Cookery** As one of the tastiest of the *Agaricus* genus and excellent for use as a vegetable, *A. arvensis* comes highly recommended. It can be employed as an accompaniment to meat dishes and is also useful as an ingredient of sauces, soups and omelettes. The size and shape of the caps make it eminently suitable for stuffing as an appetizer or a snack meal. Use the stalk cleaned and chopped into small pieces with tomato and shallot or, as an alternative, sage and onion. Another delicious recipe during the late summer uses the chopped stalk with pieces of marrow and topped off with a cheese sauce. The species is not recommended for use raw in salads.

Agaricus augustus

(Psalliota augusta)

The Prince

■ **Where and when** Another excellent member of the *Agaricus* genus, this is one of a limited number which occur in woods, both broad-leaved and coniferous. Look out for a large, handsome mushroom with a brown-flecked appearance that emerges from late summer through the autumn.

■ **Appearance** The cap is egg-shaped or ovoid at first, becoming domed or convex and finally irregularly flattened in older specimens extending to as much as 20 cm across. It is of a yellowish colour but covered with fibrous chestnut brown scales which tend to merge into a more uniform brown coloration towards the centre. The size of the stalk is in proportion with the cap and it bears a large pendulous ring towards the apex. Below the ring the stalk may be decorated with small pallid scales and it bruises yellowish. The gills are free from the stalk, at first white becoming quickly dark reddish or chocolate brown. The spores are purple-brown. The taste of *A. augustus* is strongly mushroomy though it has an aroma of almonds.

■ **Cookery** A good all-round cooked vegetable, *A. augustus* will serve as a dish in its own right, or as an accompaniment to meat dishes. Use it in omelettes, soups, casseroles and as a garnish. It is not, however, recommended raw in salads.

Agaricus bisporus

■ **Where and when** The modern shop-bought white mushroom is almost certainly descended from this wild plant which is distinguished microscopically in that its spores are arranged in groups of two instead of the more typical four, hence '*bisporus*'. It is very uncommon in the wild and the illustration is a photograph of one of the many commercial hybrids generally identified as *A. bisporus* var. *hortensis*. When it does occur it is to be found on manure heaps and amongst garden rubbish on rich humus. It does not normally grow in fields and pastures.

■ **Appearance** The colour of the caps in the wild parent is more brown than you would expect in the commercial variety, and the caps are covered in fine radiating fibres. Emerging as small buttons they expand into domed or convex and finally more or less flattened plates measuring up to 10 cm across. The stalk is white and has a membranous ring (not as pendulous as in some other species of *Agaricus*) towards its apex. The flesh tends to bruise a reddish-brown colour, particularly in older specimens. The gills are more or less free, pinkish at first but soon darkening to reddish or chocolate brown. The spores are also chocolate brown. The taste and smell are much as you would expect in a shop-bought mushroom but generally rather stronger.

In France the mushroom is known as the Champignon de Paris and it was in Paris that the technique for growing mushrooms artificially on horse manure was first established in 1707 by de Tournefort. It was not until nearly the turn of the twentieth century, however, that a reliable technique was developed to isolate pure viable mushroom spawn and the first crops were eventually grown on horse manure in cellars under the city.

Nowadays, the centre of cultivation has moved south and much of the annual crop is grown in vast limestone caverns in the Ain region north of Lyon. The modern compost is formulated from straw and pig manure, composted in long stacks where it is allowed to heat up through the activity of bacteria. The stacks are turned mechanically at intervals to keep them aerated and, after twelve days, the compost is pasteurized, cooled, capped with a special chalky layer and inoculated with mushroom spawn (the mushroom spores are impregnated into cereal grains).

■ **Cookery** The culinary virtues of *A. bisporus* need not be repeated here. It is one of the mushrooms which can be served equally well cooked or raw in a salad dish. The unopened, or partially opened, caps when the gills are still pink are better for use raw whilst the expanded caps with dark gills produce a much stronger taste in cooked dishes. In general, however, it is fair to say that the cultivated species generates milder flavours than its wild counterpart.

Agaricus campestris

(Psalliota campestris)

Common Field Mushroom

■ **Where and when** The title 'common' is, sadly, no more than a euphemism these days. The widespread loss of horses from the landscape, spraying with selective herbicides and the practice of regular crop rotation have played their part in its decline. The mushroom still appears with some frequency, if you know the right places, but it is hardly a familiar sight. *Agaricus campestris* bears no direct relationship to the shop-bought mushroom which is probably descended from a close relative, *A. bisporus*. If you are looking for *A. campestris* it appears in pastureland from mid-summer to autumn.

■ **Appearance** The caps are off-white, sometimes with a yellowish tinge, first emerging as buttons and remaining strongly bun-shaped for a long time before eventually flattening as old and often discoloured specimens. The caps may be either scaly or smooth and extend to 10 cm across. The stalk is also off-white and generally tapers towards the base. The ring is inconspicuous and often sloughs off altogether. The flesh is firm and white though bruising a reddish pink colour. The gills are deep pink, even in very young unopened caps, and they mature to dull brown or chocolate. They are more or less free from the apex of the stalk. The spores are dull brown. The smell and taste are typically mushroomy.

■ **Cookery** One of the best all-round mushrooms for the kitchen, it serves with equal gallantry as a cooked vegetable and raw in salads. Use it as you will, as an accompaniment to virtually every kind of meat and fish dish. If there is any criticism, it is that *A. campestris*, in common with the other members of the family, is not particularly striking when it comes to imparting colour to a dish. Otherwise it earns full marks and is one of the most popular wild mushrooms both in Great Britain and Continental Europe.

Agaricus macrosporus

(Psalliota arvensis subsp. *macrospora)*

■ **Where and when** This is a real giant of a mushroom and one which occurs typically growing in rings. It is, nevertheless, strictly an occasional encounter, growing in pastures and appearing during the summer and autumn months.

■ **Appearance** The caps emerge as sizeable buttons and remain bun-shaped for a long time before expanding into massive, domed plates which can be as much as 40 cm across. They make a dramatic sight in a field, like so many white flying saucers. The cap surface breaks up into cream-coloured scales and the margin may become a little ragged with age. The cap rests on a massive swollen stalk which tapers at the base and is covered, in its lower half, with thick woolly scales which are readily sloughed off. The ring is thick, white and pendulous though in most cases the mushroom is picked when the cap is still closed and the veil intact. The gills are at first flesh-coloured, turning dark brown with age and the spores are brown.

Some authors suggest that this species smells of almonds and, in older fruiting bodies, of ammonia. In my experience this is incorrect. Regardless of age, the *A. macrosporus* specimens I have collected smell only of aniseed.

■ **Cookery** This is an excellent mushroom for cooking and a firm personal favourite which I have to rate as one of the most delicious tasting of the *Agaricus* genus. A good-sized mushroom makes a meal in itself and since it often occurs gregariously in rings, *A. macrosporus* can provide for a large dinner party! The taste is quite strong with an almost peppery bite and the texture is quite different to that of *A. campestris*; it is much more solid. As a vegetable in its own right, the mushroom is best prepared by cutting it into manageable chunks (the cap and stalk are equally palatable) because the fruiting bodies really do grow to a massive size. If one attempts to cook the caps or stalks whole the centres may be left raw.

This is a species probably not to be recommended for use in salads though it should be stressed that it will cause no harm if eaten uncooked.

Agaricus silvicola

(Psalliota sylvicola)

Wood Mushroom

■ **Where and when** This is a mushroom which needs to be identified with care. It is a medium to large species, not particularly fleshy, found in both coniferous and broad-leaved woodlands throughout the autumn until the first frosts.

■ **Appearance** The caps are smooth and cream-coloured but they bruise yellowish. They are domed or convex when they first emerge, expanding to broad inverted saucers measuring up to 10 cm across. The stalk is in proportion with the cap, of similar colour, typically with a bulbous base and with a prominent pendulous ring towards the apex. The flesh is white. The gills are a pallid dirty pink at first, becoming chocolate brown with age and they are free from the stalk. The spores are purple brown. The fruiting bodies smell distinctly of aniseed and taste mushroomy.

One needs to be aware of a closely related species, *A. xanthodermus* which is poisonous though not deadly. Size, coloration and general appearance are similar and both occur in autumn woods. There are two essential clues to help distinguish the species. First, smell the mushroom. If it possesses an unpleasant aroma of ink and definitely does not smell of aniseed it is probably *A. xanthodermus*. Secondly, using a sharp knife, slice down the stalk lengthwise. In *A. xanthodermus* the extreme base (the bulbous area) will rapidly turn chrome yellow. This will not happen with *A. silvicola*. If the two are confused, the worst effects of eating are sweating and stomach cramps but it is better to avoid the experience.

■ **Cookery** This is another excellent edible member of the *Agaricus* genus. Good for use as a side dish or an appetizer, *A. silvicola* lends itself ideally as an accompaniment to meat dishes and its flavour also comes through well in soups, sauces and omelettes.

Agaricus silvaticus

(Psalliota sylvatica)

■ **Where and when** This is another woodland species of the *Agaricus* genus. Not unlike *A. augustus* on first inspection, this is a medium to large fleshy mushroom limited to coniferous areas and making an appearance from mid-summer until the first frosts.

■ **Appearance** The cap is button-like to begin with, expanding to domed or convex but less often saucer-shaped and up to 10 cm across. The surface is broken up into small, brown, fibrous scales through which the pallid whitish background flesh is visible. The stalk is dirty white and bears a pendulous brownish ring towards the apex. The base is generally slightly bulbous. The flesh throughout the fruiting body flushes a distinctive reddish colour when cut. The gills are at first pallid flesh-colour, maturing to dark brown, and the spores are brown. The taste and smell are not distinctive.

■ **Cookery** Perhaps the weakest member of the *Agaricus* genus for the table, if only because aroma and flavour are unremarkable, it can still provide a reasonable meal. Use these mushrooms in the same way as is recommended for *A. augustus* but don't wait for your taste buds to explode with excitement. The species is probably on a culinary par with *A. bisporus* but finding it necessitates a lot more effort than popping down to the supermarket!

Coprinus atramentarius

Common Ink Cap

■ **Where and when** A large member of the ink cap family, *C. atramentarius* appears in a wide variety of places from woodlands to roadside verges and even can be found poking up through tarmac drives. It grows from submerged rotten wood. Often clumped together, the fruiting bodies emerge in greatest concentrations in autumn but can often be discovered from the spring months onwards. The species is extremely common.

■ **Appearance** The caps are egg-shaped or ovoid at first, soon expanding into broad cones which are radially wrinkled and finally split lengthwise. These cones can be up to 7 cm high. The colour is generally a dirty yellowish brown, paling at the margin. Like certain other *Coprinus* fungi, *C. atramentarius* sheds and disperses its spores by a process of autodigestion. The flesh decomposes, from the margin inwards, into an inky black fluid which is then spread by the feet of passing animals. In old specimens a remnant of the cap is left as a central disc, the edges of which are upturned.

The stalk is quite thick, smooth and white (though often discoloured blackish by autodigestion products). It may have a ring-like zone near the base. The gills are crowded, at first pallid or off-white, then turning black from the edges towards the cap and finally deliquescing or dissolving into black fluid. The spores are brown. There is little smell and taste.

■ **Cookery** *Coprinus atramentarius* is edible and good but with certain reservations that are ignored at one's peril! This mushroom provides a good illustration of the maxim 'do not eat without reading the instructions'. The main problem about eating *C. atramentarius* is the effect of combining the fungus with alcohol. It synthesizes a complex chemical substance which is soluble in alcohol and which causes adverse symptoms including nausea, sweating, flushing and alarming palpitations. Essentially, providing no alcohol is consumed within 24 hours before or after the meal, *C. atramentarius* makes an edible dish! Be advised though, the Continental experts give it only a modest one-star rating in most '*champignons comestibles*' lists.

Coprinus comatus

Shaggy Ink Cap; Judge's Wig

■ **Where and when** This delightful mushroom grows prolifically in the mown grass of roadside verges, often in large scattered groups, but is also to be found in lawns and on garden rubbish heaps.

■ **Appearance** A tall elegant fungus when at its peak of growth; the caps are at first egg-shaped or ovoid and, from a distance, appear pure white covered with large shaggy scales whose tips soon become tinted brown. The apex is generally brownish-coloured and smooth. As they mature the caps become conical, up to 15 cm tall, and they darken from the margin. Like *C. atramentarius*, *C. comatus* sheds and disperses its spores by a process of autodigestion. The flesh decomposes, from the margin inwards, into an inky black fluid which is then spread by the feet of passing animals. In old specimens a remnant of the cap is left as a central disc, the edges of which are upturned.

The stalk is tall and white, though it may be stained with the products of autodigestion. It bears a thin white ring which often becomes loosened and which then slips to the base. The gills are crowded, at first pallid or off-white, turning pinkish and finally black from the edges towards the cap, deliquescing or dissolving into black fluid. The spores are brown. There is little smell and taste.

■ **Cookery** This species displays none of the risky characteristics of the Common Ink Cap and makes one of the most delicate wild fungus meals imaginable. It is well worth collecting for the table. When you have collected the mushrooms, open them up and discard any that have matured beyond a pale pink in the gills. It is not necessary to scrape away the shaggy scales unless they have become thoroughly begrimed. They add a pretty decorative texture.

Use *C. comatus* especially in fresh salads where, as a raw ingredient, it will lend a delicate flavour. Slice the caps lengthways and add them as a decorative addition. If the mushroom is to be cooked as a dish in its own right, then it requires only the most delicate sauté followed perhaps by the boost of a little medium white wine and a pinch of nutmeg. It requires the gentlest of baking in the oven. Serve with croutons.

Coprinus micaceus

■ **Where and when** This is another very common ink cap and, although smaller than *C. atramentarius* or *C. comatus*, it generally grows in dense tufts often of a hundred or more, on stumps or buried wood of broad-leaved trees. The fruiting bodies emerge over a long period of the year from late spring to early winter.

■ **Appearance** The caps are dull ochre yellow turning to cinnamon brown towards the centre and, generally speaking, they become more overall brown colour as they age. Particularly when young, they are covered with tiny mica-like particles, the remnants of the veil which covered the cap as it emerged through the ground. These velar fragments may give the cap a faintly glistening appearance. At first each cap is egg-shaped or ovoid but as it expands it becomes conical, measuring up to 4 cm high, and is wrinkled radially.

The stalk is off-white becoming more buff-coloured lower down. There is no obvious ring. The flesh is white. The gills are off-white turning brown and finally black as they mature. The spores are brown and distributed by autodigestion. The flesh decomposes, from the margin of the cap inwards, into an inky black fluid which is then spread by the feet of passing animals. Very often one comes across a black gooey mess, barely recognizable, on a stump which is all that remains of a once prolific colony of *C. micaceus* fruiting bodies.

■ **Cookery** It is important to stress that, once on the kitchen table, the specimens should be inspected and any about which there is a hint of decomposition should be discarded. The species is not recommended for use raw in salads, and is best cooked, with a gentle sauté, as a dish in its own right.

Hypholoma capnoides

■ **Where and when** This is an uncommon species of edible fungus which is nevertheless worthwhile if one comes across it because it usually grows in tufts including large numbers of specimens. It emerges on conifer stumps. The fruiting bodies also appear throughout a large part of the year, from spring to the first frosts, although they are always difficult to find.

■ **Appearance** The caps are small to medium in size, but they are quite fleshy. Pallid ochre yellow flushing tan towards the centre, they may be decorated with slightly darker flecks. In profile they are domed or convex almost from the outset, emerging with a slight central hump or umbo. Each cap extends to a maximum diameter of 6 cm. The stalk is buff-coloured with ochre yellow tinges and is flushed reddish at the base. Beneath the cap is a whiter zone. The flesh is yellowish. The gills are pallid at first, becoming greyish brown with a lilac tinge. The spores are dark brown. The taste and smell are not particularly distinctive.

■ **Cookery** There is nothing much to note about *H. capnoides*. It is quite safe to eat and it probably claims a one-star palatability rating. Not to be recommended for use raw, it is worth trying as a cooked mushroom if you come across it. It may leave you wildly ecstatic but I doubt it.

Bovista plumbea

■ **Where and when** These small white puffballs, members of the Gasteromycete group, are locally common in Britain particularly in the north and west of England appearing on lawns and amongst short grass from late summer and through the autumn. Elsewhere they are infrequent. Each autumn a crop of them appears scattered across my garden lawn.

■ **Appearance** The fruiting body takes the form of a sub-spherical white ball, about 3 cm across, which is slightly pointed underneath and extends into mycelial cords which attach it to the underground mycelium. When young the ball is quite firm to the touch and more or less smooth, though the surface of the outer wall may start to flake. The fertile tissue generating the spores, the gleba, is contained inside. At first this is also white and fairly solid but, as the spores mature, the mass of the gleba darkens to olive green or brown. The spores are brown when isolated. Finally, the wall breaks open irregularly to release the spores, the top of the ball fragments and finally a brown papery bowl is all that remains. This may persist in the grass, often detaching from the mycelium and blowing about loose, for several weeks or months. Even in the late spring it is still possible to come across the remnants when mowing the grass.

■ **Cookery** On the plate these little puffballs are not unlike their overgrown cousin, *Langermannia gigantea*, and are firm and tasty. Not to be recommended for drying, they are best halved and gently sautéed. *Bovista plumbea* also pickles well.

Calvatia excipuliformis

(Lycoperdon excipuliformis)

■ **Where and when** Amongst the common edible puffballs this is one of the easiest to recognize on account of its shape and colour. It is found growing on soil in a wide variety of places from woodlands, to heaths, pastures and urban wasteground during the autumn months.

■ **Appearance** The fruiting body is pestle-shaped, pallid buff at first but gradually darkening to dull brown. The upper fertile section is up to 20 cm high and 10 cm across, though usually smaller, and rests on top of a sterile stalk zone. The wall containing the spore mass consists of two layers, the outer of which is warty but soon flakes away to reveal a smooth inner wrapping.

When mature, the inner fertile tissue generating the spores is dark purple brown and the papery wall breaks open to release the spores, which are olive brown. The infertile base of the pedestal, when cut open, reveals a spongy brown tissue. The bases of the fruiting bodies are remarkably resistant and can stay around for months after discharging their spores, looking like weird flat-topped ice-cream cones filled with a soggy mass of brown spores.

■ **Cookery** The suggestions given for *Langermannia* are equally applicable bearing in mind that it will take several of these smaller fruiting bodies to equal one Giant Puffball.

Langermannia gigantea

(Calvatia gigantea)

Giant Puffball

I have a vivid recollection of the first time I saw one of these extraordinary plants. Probably one of the most dramatic of all fungi in appearance, the species is capable of achieving impressive statistics and is delicious to eat.

■ **Where and when** Sadly quite uncommon, *L. gigantea* does occur in reasonable numbers in certain locations around the country. It tends to be a summer rather than an autumn species though it can make its appearance as late as October. The fruiting bodies grow on soil in nettle beds, field borders and waste ground.

■ **Appearance** The unripe fruiting body is white thoughout, leathery, and sub-spherical and attached by a few mycelial cords. It can grow up to 80 cm across. As the spore-bearing tissue, the gleba, ripens it darkens in colour and eventually the outer wall of the fruiting body splits open to liberate the rusty brown spore mass. When this happens the whole puffball often breaks loose from the underground mycelium and rolls about in the wind, thus scattering the millions of spores more effectively. The spores are brown.

■ **Cookery** In times gone by, country people would go in search of the Giant Puffball as a great delicacy. The Freemasons Tavern in London even served them up as a *pièce de résistance* on state occasions. Now, sadly, they are more likely to be kicked to pieces as objects of distrust.

Whichever way you care to prepare the fungi, it is essential that they are sliced open and checked for colour. They must be white all the way through. In *Food in England* Dorothy Hartley recalls several delightful, if largely forgotten, recipes for these extraordinary growths. The traditional method of preparation is to cut the puffball into slices like a loaf of bread, dip the slices into beaten egg and coat with breadcrumbs. The crumbs need to be pressed in firmly and the slices put aside on a covered plate for a hour or so. The coated slices are then sautéed in butter, turning once, seasoned and served with a dash of lemon juice. The texture is vaguely reminiscent of sweetbreads and the flavour is delicate and slightly nutty.

An alternative suggestion is to cut the top from the puffball and hollow it out, as if it were a melon. Chop up the flesh taken from the centre, brown it in butter with a few finely chopped shallots, and add a small can of chestnut stuffing. Spoon the mixture back into the shell, replace the lid and top with strips of streaky bacon. Wrap the puffball in foil and bake in a moderate oven for 45 minutes. Devastating!

Lycoperdon perlatum

(Lycoperdon gemmatum)

■ **Where and when** Amongst the commonest of the puffballs, *L. perlatum* can be found growing on soil in woods throughout the summer and autumn months.

■ **Appearance** The unripe fruiting body is white and shaped like a squat pestle. The upper part is sub-spherical, extends to 6 cm across, and rests on top of a distinct stalk zone. The fertile spore-bearing tissue, the gleba, is enclosed in the upper section by a two-layered wall. In the young unripe puffball the outer layer is decorated with small warty fragments which slough off to leave an irregular pattern on the surface of the papery inner layer. As the spores ripen, the gleba turns brown and the retaining wall becomes pallid brown opening by a pore near the top to release the spores. These are expelled by the impact of raindrops, or passing feet, on the now papery container. The spores are olive brown. The stalk is sterile and filled with spongy tissue.

■ **Cookery** Most of the small puffballs are edible and good to eat though they need to be collected in reasonable quantities to make a meal. It is, however, important to appreciate that there are also certain species with which puffballs might be confused. The Earth Ball (*Scleroderma citrinum*), which is harder and more yellowish in colour, is definitely to be avoided. The unopened eggs of the Stinkhorn (*Phallus impudicus*) are also not dissimilar but have a much smoother and more rubbery feel. These latter specimens are harmless but might give you a surprise when you cut into them!

Lycoperdon pyriforme

■ **Where and when** This is an easy puffball to spot because it is the only commonly encountered species which grows on wood. Sometimes large numbers can be found massed on rotting stumps and logs. They may appear to be growing on soil but close inspection will reveal that the mycelial cords are connected with buried wood. *Lycoperdon pyriforme* appears from late summer through the autumn and is widespread.

■ **Appearance** The unripe fruiting body is sub-spherical or club-shaped and white. The upper fertile part extends to 4 cm across and rests on top of a sterile stalk zone. The fertile spore-bearing tissue, the gleba, is enclosed in the upper section by a two-layered wall. In the young unripe puffball the outer layer is decorated with small scurfy fragments which slough off to expose the smooth papery inner layer. As the spores ripen, the gleba turns brown and the retaining wall becomes greyish brown, opening by a pore near the top to release the spores. These are expelled by the impact of raindrops, or passing feet, on the now papery container. The spores are olive brown. The stalk is sterile and filled with spongy tissue.

■ **Cookery** As with *L. perlatum*, beware of possible confusion with *Scleroderma* or *Phallus*. The taste and texture are similar to other puffballs.

Vascellum pratense

■ **Where and when** Particularly common on garden lawns and other areas of mown grass including golf courses, it is often possible to collect enough of these puffballs to make a good meal. They appear from mid-summer until the first frosts. With *Bovista* this is one of the species that regularly emerges in my own garden.

■ **Appearance** The unripe fruiting body is white, sub-spherical, and extends to 4 cm across. The upper fertile part narrows into a sterile basal region connected with the underground mycelium. The fertile spore-bearing tissue, the gleba, is enclosed in the upper section by a two-layered wall. In the young unripe puffball the outer layer is decorated with small scurfy fragments and spines which slough off to expose the smooth papery inner layer. As the spores ripen, the gleba turns brown and the retaining wall becomes pallid brown, opening by a regular pore near the top to release the spores. These are expelled by the impact of raindrops, or passing feet, on the now papery container. Eventually the whole of the upper part of the wall breaks away, leaving a ragged bowl. The spores are olive brown. The stalk is sterile and filled with spongy tissue.

■ **Cookery** Treat *V. pratense* in the same way as other puffballs and with the same reservations about confusion with lookalikes.

Phallus impudicus

Stinkhorn

This is probably the surprise inclusion in the list, but for the dedicated fungus gourmet it really does have to be mentioned.

■ **Where and when** One is definitely guided to Stinkhorns by one's nose. The immature 'eggs' can be found partially buried in leaf litter, frequently growing under conifers and often in sizeable numbers. They are also to be discovered in gardens and mixed woodlands.

■ **Appearance** Each 'egg' is off-white, with a leathery surface, a squashy feel, and is up to 6 cm across. (*Note*: the eggs illustrated here appear disproportionately large compared to the mature fruiting body shown.) Inside is a thick, semi-transparent jelly surrounding the embryo stalk and cap. The egg is attached to the underground mycelium by a little white cord.

When the egg reaches a stage of maturity, it cracks open and a thick white spongy stalk pushes rapidly upwards carrying a bell-shaped cap covered

Phallus impudicus: mature fruiting body.

in dark olive green slime which contains the spores. During the course of a day, flies are attracted to the slime by the stench of rotting meat and they gradually remove it, leaving a ribbed white remnant which may then persist for a further day or two. The spores stick to the legs of the insects and are thus distributed.

■ **Cookery** The expanded fruiting body, the part which smells so repellent, is inedible for obvious reasons. The immature egg, however, carries none of the foul odour of the ripe specimen, and is edible though not particularly tasty. It is reputed to possess aphrodisiac properties but this quality is almost certainly little more than a piece of folklore stimulated by the provocative shape of the fungus when in its prime. Please judge for yourself, however. The experience will cause no harm and may even be enlightening!

Auricularia auricula-judae

(Hirneola auricula-judae)

Jew's Ear

■ **Where and when** This is an attractive-looking edible fungus which grows almost exclusively on the trunks and branches of elder trees (*Sambucus nigra*) though it does sometimes appear on other deciduous wood. The fruiting bodies can be found throughout the year, though predominantly in the late summer and autumn months, and it is extremely common.

■ **Appearance** The fruiting body is shaped like an ear, showing vein-like markings. It is partly wrinkled, points downwards and grows up to 8 cm across. The colour is uniformly tan brown, sometimes with greyish tinges, slightly velvety on the outer (upper) surface and smoothly polished on the inner (lower) surface. In damp or wet weather the texture is rubbery or gelatinous. In dry conditions the fungus shrivels to a darkish tough leathery lump, but has the remarkable capacity to revive and reconstitute when wetted. The spores are white.

■ **Cookery** One needs a sharp knife to remove the fruiting bodies which are firmly attached to the bark of the host and which tend to tear. It does not work to sauté them in butter as they become very tough in the process. The best approach is slow and gentle cooking in milk or stock in a casserole. The texture is crisp but very palatable and the flavour is retained. Alternatively, the caps can be cut into pieces and very quickly stir-fried with vegetables in the Cantonese manner. A similar variety is actually grown on a commercial scale in China using wooden palings.

Lentinellus cochleatus

Ear Fungus

■ **Where and when** An unusual and easily recognizable fungus, *L. cochleatus* grows in small tufts on stumps of broad-leaved trees during the autumn months. It is uncommon.

■ **Appearance** *Lentinellus cochleatus* is one of the species that cannot make up its mind whether it is a mushroom or a bracket. It grows as a funnel-shaped cap with an off-centre stalk. The fruiting body is reddish brown and smooth on the upper surface. The stalk is similarly coloured in its upper half but darkens to a more chestnut brown towards the base. The flesh is pale pink. The gills are strongly decurrent (running down the stalk), pallid flesh-coloured, and produce white spores. The fungus has a distinctive aroma of aniseed and the taste is not distinctive.

■ **Cookery** Not an inspiring specimen for the table, the texture is good and the aniseed smell puts *L. cochleatus* in line for a modest two-star rating. It is best gently sautéed.

Pleurotus cornucopiae

(Pleurotus sapidus)

■ **Where and when** This is a dramatic-looking specimen which can make an appearance throughout the warmer months of the year, from spring to autumn, springing in large clusters from a log or stump, but it is infrequent in occurrence. It usually favours elm or oak as a host plant.

■ **Appearance** The cap is large, fleshy and eccentric on the stalk, at first convex, expanding into a shallow funnel or shell-shape and extending up to 12 cm across. It is cream-coloured, often with a white bloom in the early stages of growth. As it ages it becomes progressively more yellowed and finally brownish yellow, often with a wavy outline, and the margin tends to split. The stalk is concolorous with the cap or paler and typically several fruiting bodies arise from a common base. The flesh is white and rubbery firm. The gills are strongly decurrent, running down the stalk, slightly paler than the cap colour and the spores are pale lilac.

The fruiting bodies have a mealy smell and the taste is not distinctive.

■ **Cookery** A first-class fungus for the pan, *P. cornucopiae* makes an excellent meal if picked reasonably fresh. The comments given for *P. ostreatus* also apply to this species though it is perhaps not quite so prized as *P. ostreatus* in terms of flavour and texture.

Pleurotus ostreatus

Oyster Cap

■ **Where and when** Of similar size to *P. cornucopiae*, the fruiting bodies can occur throughout the year typically in dramatic clusters on fallen timber or stumps of deciduous trees. It favours beech as a host plant.

■ **Appearance** The cap is large, fleshy and eccentric on the stalk, at first convex expanding into a shallow funnel or shell-shape, often with a wavy outline, and extending up to 14 cm across. The colour varies through brownish to blue-grey, turning a more dull brown with age. The surface is smooth and appears fibrous and the margin tends to split with age. The stalk is off-centre or lateral and may be quite long, very short, or absent altogether. It is white and smooth except at the base which tends to be woolly. The gills are strongly decurrent, running down the stalk, crowded together, white when young then tinged yellowish-cream. The spores are pale lilac. The taste and smell are not distinctive.

■ **Cookery** This is another first-rate discovery for the table. It is firm-fleshed and grows to a substantial size. A few years ago *P. ostreatus* was only viewed with enthusiasm by intrepid connoisseurs in the British Isles though it has long been esteemed in Continental Europe. That attitude is now beginning to change and it is encouraging to see an increasing number of British chefs including it amongst their mushroom dishes.

It is certainly worthy of acclaim. Perhaps one of the drawbacks to sensitive eyes is the colour: after all, whoever heard of eating blue vegetables! The flesh is fairly rubbery and needs careful cooking but Oyster Cap has a fine strong flavour and is full of delicious juice. It has a slight peppery tang.

One of my own favourite recipes demands a lemon sauce. The stalks are discarded and caps are sliced into convenient pieces. These are then browned slightly in a little olive oil with a handful of chopped shallot. Transfer to a baking dish and just cover the fungus and shallot with half water, half dry white wine, season, and bake until tender (about 30 minutes). Add the juice of a lemon and a little thickening (cornflour) and return to the oven for 5 minutes before serving. The lemon definitely enhances the flavour of the Oyster Cap and gives the dish a pleasant piquancy.

Boletus badius

(Xerocomus badius)

Bay Bolete

■ **Where and when** This is one of the easily recognizable of the *Boletus* genus, all of which have the casual appearance of an agaric mushroom but with the gills replaced by tubes opening through small pores on the underside of the cap. *Boletus badius* is a large species common in coniferous woodlands through the autumn months growing on soil. It can also appear under broad-leaved trees.

■ **Appearance** The cap is a distinctive bay brown colour, bun-shaped, the surface at first slightly velvety then smooth and with a polished appearance, becoming sticky or viscid in wet weather. It can extend to 12 cm across. The stalk is of similar colour to the cap, with a striated cottony surface, finely woolly at the base. The flesh is lemon yellow, firm and full. The cut flesh turns faintly blue immediately above the tubes. The pores are large, pale cream at first becoming more lemon yellow, turning rapidly blue-green where bruised. The spores are olive brown.

■ **Cookery** The majority of boletes are safe to eat but, as a general rule, any with reddish-coloured spores should be avoided. Members of this family of fungi have been considered a delicacy since the time of the Romans although their system of naming seems designed to confuse us. To a Roman gourmet, the gill-bearing fungi were 'boleti' and what we now recognize as boletes were 'suilli' (Latin: *suillus* 'of pigs') on account of the preferences of Roman pigs which apparently tucked into them with gusto. The Roman cook would prepare the fungi by stewing them in a stock fortified with a salty extract of fish guts, or *liquamen*, and ground pepper. They also served them raw with a pepper, olive oil and vinegar dressing.

Nowadays, boletes are collected on a commercial scale and either marketed for home consumption or exported from Italy, Czechoslovakia, Russia, Germany and Poland.

There are a few general rules to observe when picking boletes for the table. With few exceptions the species are edible and good. As a family, however, they do tend to become worm- or maggot-infested very quickly, particularly in warm damp weather. It is essential to select only young specimens that feel firm, are not discoloured, and do not have obvious bore holes. It is not necessary to remove either skin or pores and some species are eminently suitable for use raw in salads.

Boletus edulis

Cep; Penny Bun

■ **Where and when** On the Continent this is one of the best known and most sought-after of all the edible fungi. Not uncommon in certain areas, its great popularity may have resulted in a decline in recent years. The fruiting bodies can grow to an impressive size. They make their appearance throughout the summer and autumn months in woodlands of all kinds, though predominantly under broad-leaved trees, particularly favouring beech.

■ **Appearance** The cap is bun-shaped, expanding to 20 cm or more across and it is brown and smooth. At first it may have a whitish bloom but later it develops a smooth polished appearance. In wet weather the surface can feel sticky or viscid. The stalk is typically massive and swollen, pallid brown in colour, the surface decorated with a fine white mesh of 'veins'. The flesh is white and firm and does not change colour when cut. The pores are fine, rounded in cross-section, and are dirty white in colour later with a yellowish tinge. They do not bruise blue or green. The spores are brown. The taste and smell are not distinctive.

■ **Cookery** The redoubtable Victorian mushroom picker and gourmet, the Reverend Worthington Smith describes the Cep in glowing terms: 'one of the most delicious and tender objects of food ever submitted to the operation of cooking'. I would have to agree with him!

Looking around Europe, one finds many local recipes, for example, there is a traditional Hungarian soup made from dried Ceps. The caps are soaked overnight in water and toasted bread is added. When the mixture takes on the consistency of a purée it is pressed through a sieve. A number of previously stewed whole caps are added and the soup is simmered gently for a further 5 minutes before serving.

The classic modern Italian recipes call for the caps to be separated from the stalks, laid upsidedown, seasoned and doused with melted butter. The caps are then baked in the oven until tender.

Apart from its well-earned reputation in the kitchen, it was claimed by United States research workers in the 1930s that *B. edulis* had notable inhibitory properties for certain types of cancer. Unfortunately, it has never been possible to exploit or fully evaluate the claims since no technique has been discovered to grow *B. edulis* on a large-scale commercial basis.

Boletus erythropus

■ **Where and when** The large fleshy caps appear on soil under trees generally, both coniferous and broad-leaved, from late summer onwards until the first frosts. It is a common species.

■ **Appearance** The cap is bun-shaped and expands to as much as 20 cm across. It is brown or bay brown in colour with olive tinges and may show a thin yellowish margin. At first it may be velvety but it soon becomes smooth. It may feel a little sticky or viscid in wet weather. The stalk is massive, club-shaped and covered with a decoration of dense red dots over a yellowish background. The flesh is yellow but rapidly turns blue-black where cut. The pores are fine, rounded in cross-section, orange-red, later more brownish red, rapidly turning blue-black where bruised. The spores are olive brown. The taste and smell are not distinctive.

■ **Cookery** This is a species which is edible and good but which needs to be approached with caution because of possible confusion with poisonous members of the family. It can be treated in much the same way as *B. edulis*.

Boletus parasiticus

(Xerocomus parasiticus)

■ **Where and when** Although very uncommon, this species is instantly recognizable because it grows in unique circumstances as a parasite on the Common Earth Ball, *Scleroderma citrinum*. It appears during the autumn months and is one of the smaller members of the *Boletus* genus.

■ **Appearance** The cap is bun-shaped or, more typically, irregular in profile, extending to 4 cm across, yellowish brown in colour usually with an olive tinge. The surface may be slightly downy and soon becomes crazed. The stalk is cap-coloured, tapers downwards, and usually curves around and up from the base of the *Scleroderma*. The flesh is pallid yellow with rusty brown tinges at the base of the stalk. It does not change colour when cut. The pores are yellow becoming olive brown with age, sometimes with reddish patches and may run slightly down the stalk (decurrent). They do not bruise to a distinctive colour. The spores are olive brown. The taste and smell are not distinctive.

■ **Cookery** This species can be prepared and cooked much as *B. edulis* but it is not the most inspiring of edible boletes.

Suillus bovinus

(Boletus bovinus)

■ **Where and when** A third group of *Boletus*-like fungi, the *Suillus* genus has slimy or glutinous caps. *Suillus bovinus* is a fleshy, medium-sized species which appears commonly on soil in conifer woods, generally with Scots pines, during the autumn months.

■ **Appearance** The cap is convex, becoming more or less flattened and expanding up to 10 cm across, buff-coloured often with pinkish tinges but paler in a distinct thin zone around the margin. The surface is smooth and slimy or sticky. The stalk is more or less cap-coloured and typically tapers towards the base. The flesh is pale yellowish pink, more rusty brown in the stalk. The pores are large, angular, slightly decurrent (running down the stalk), the tubes dividing into smaller passages beneath the surface. The pores are buff at first then more ochre yellow and finally yellowish brown. The spores are olive brown. The taste is sweet and the flesh has a fruity aroma.

■ **Cookery** The biggest problem in preparing any of the *Suillus* fungi lies in the fact that the slime acts as a 'magnet' for dust, flies and grit, all of which has to be removed. I would suggest peeling; any surplus slime is then easily removed under the tap. Like most of the *Suillus* genus, *S. bovinus* is edible, pleasant, but unremarkable. One can often collect it in reasonable quantities and it is probably best employed in soups, casseroles and sauces. It is not suitable for drying or freezing because the flesh is too moist.

Suillus granulatus

(Boletus granulatus)

■ **Where and when** This is a common and quite distinctive medium-sized edible species which appears on soil under conifers in late autumn.

■ **Appearance** The cap is convex, becoming more or less flattened and expanding up to 10 cm across, rusty yellow. The surface is smooth and slimy or sticky. The stalk is pallid yellow flushing to a pinkish red towards the base and adjacent to the cap it bears a granular surface which oozes characteristic milky drops. The flesh is pale lemon yellow, almost white in the cap and does not change colour when cut. The pores are yellow, also discharging milky fluid, and becoming tinged olive with age. There is no obvious colour change when they are bruised. The taste and smell are not distinctive.

■ **Cookery** One of those 'middling' species which is not really exciting on the taste buds, but available in reasonable quantity and which will provide a useful addition to soups, casseroles and sauces. They are not suitable for drying or freezing.

Suillus grevillei

(Boletus elegans)

Larch Bolete

■ **Where and when** This is an extremely common species with a distinctive appearance. The fruiting bodies emerge from late summer onwards until the first frosts and occur only in association with larches, which makes *S. grevillei* an easy fungus to identify.

■ **Appearance** The cap is convex becoming more or less flattened and expanding up to 10 cm across, bright chrome yellow becoming a yellowish-rust colour with age. The surface is smooth and slimy or sticky. The stalk is brownish yellow below a white or pale yellow membranous ring. Above the ring it is yellow. The flesh is yellow, paler in the cap than the stalk. The pores are angular, yellow at first but ageing brownish yellow, and the spores are ochre brown. The taste and smell are not distinctive.

■ **Cookery** As in the case of the other *Suillus* fungi, I would not go out of my way to recommend this specimen for the table, but if you can find enough caps they go adequately in soups, casseroles and sauces. It is not suitable for drying or freezing.

Suillus luteus

(Boletus luteus)

Slippery Jack

■ **Where and when** A large, striking, edible fungus, easily distinguished and common, *S. luteus* appears during the autumn months on soil with conifers, particularly Scots pine.

■ **Appearance** The cap first appears bun-shaped then more expanded, extending to 10 cm across, chestnut or duller brown becoming more rusty brown with age. The surface is smooth and covered with a thick coating of slimy or sticky gluten. When dry it has a polished appearance. The stalk is white, discolouring brown below the large distinctive ring which is white at first becoming brown as the fruiting body matures. Above the ring the stalk is yellow and peppered with dark granules. The cut flesh is white and firm but showing a pinkish or wine tinge at the base of the stalk. The pores are rounded in cross-section and lemon yellow, typically covered with a fine white veil in young specimens which ruptures as the cap expands. The spores are pallid or ochre yellow. The taste and smell are not distinctive.

■ **Cookery** The advice given for *S. bovinus* can be followed here.

Suillus variegatus

■ **Where and when** This is a large, fleshy *Boletus*-type fungus although not particularly frequent in occurrence. It grows on soil and the most likely spots to find it are amongst conifers. *Suillus variegatus* tends to be a species of late summer; the fruiting bodies are unlikely to appear after mid-September.

■ **Appearance** The cap is convex and can expand up to 13 cm across. It is dull yellowish brown in colour, sometimes with an olive tinge, and covered with small darker brown scales. In young specimens the surface may feel slightly velvety but it becomes slimy or sticky with age, particularly in wet weather. The stalk is ochre yellow above, becoming more yellowish brown towards the base. The flesh is yellow, pale in the cap, but deeper in the base of the stalk. It may also develop a faint blue tinge where cut, particularly above the tubes in the cap. The pores are yellowish olive in young specimens, becoming more cinnamon brown with age and are slightly angular in cross-section. Beneath the surface the tubes divide into smaller passages. The pores turn bluish where bruised. The taste is not distinctive. The smell is strongly fungal.

■ **Cookery** The advice given for *S. bovinus* applies.

Preparation and Cooking

Cooking fungi must surely be one of the more delightful adventures in the kitchen. An altogether new experience of colour, texture, flavour and aroma awaits anyone who dares to take the opportunity. If the principles of collecting fungi are followed sensibly, it is all perfectly safe. There are perhaps two golden rules to remember: never eat anything unless you are sure that it is edible and never accept wild fungi to eat from anyone who is not an acknowledged expert until you are absolutely confident of your own abilities in identification.

One of the first questions which tends to be asked is: what is the best way to cook mushrooms? The short answer is any way that you think best at the moment. They are amongst the most versatile of all vegetables and the only reservation is that very few of them require more than the briefest of cooking. Sometimes it is worth thinking of the mushrooms as your *pièce de résistance* and building the rest of the meal around them. For instance, if you have just collected a basketful of Trompettes de Mort, you may be looking at a white fish to go with them.

Because the structure of the fruiting body is made of microscopic tubes or hyphae which frequently lack the toughness of the tissue of many green plants they need to be softened hardly at all. I have watched such artists in mushroom cuisine as *cordon bleu* chef David Chambers, and they tend to apply fierce heat to the raw material for seconds rather than minutes.

There are, however, important steps to take before the mushrooms reach the pan. They require correct attention and the first priority is to go through them again. Mushrooms are not the most robust of vegetables and they really do demand prompt attention to avoid the less desirable moulds, mildews, maggots and other sundry visitors. Having said that, the place for thorough inspection is not the forest floor but the kitchen table. First make sure that everything is as fresh as possible and tallies with the appropriate description. In general, fungi that are really fresh should have a firm feel but be prepared for exceptions of texture. Not everything emulates the characteristics of the familiar commercial mushroom. Boletes that are perfectly wholesome may still have a spongy feel whilst Chanterelles are definitely elastic to the touch. It is well worthwhile taking a judicious appraisal of the freshness of the mushrooms when you are deciding how to use them. One can get away with incorporating specimens that are a little limp in a soup or casserole even if they are past their best for sautéeing. Older specimens may serve adequately for drying or pickling, whilst they look decidedly unappetizing sliced raw into a salad. In other words, common sense applies.

Resist the temptation to try and get your basketful of mushrooms squeaky clean. They are much better kept dirty and dry until immediately before you want to use them. The natural inclination is also to wash the whole mushrooms under the tap. This, however, is not the most efficient method of removing bits of soil and grit which thus far have resisted attempts to dislodge them.

If you have not already done so, first cut off the base of the stalk and discard it, or cut off the entire stalk and throw it away in those species like the large *Lepiota* species whose stalks are tough and inedible. If the stalk is to be used in cookery cut it from the cap close to the gills, or whatever structure there happens to be on the underside of the cap. Generally speaking, the stalks are best chopped into small pieces for use in fillings or in the preparation of an accompanying sauce. In any event, they can be conveniently washed whilst still in one piece. Shake off surplus water and preferably dry on a clean kitchen towel or absorbent paper. It is unlikely that the stalks will need peeling but if at the stage when you are ready to use them they appear badly discoloured or feel uncharacteristically spongy they are best thrown out. In other words, use only those in which the flesh feels firm and fairly dry and is of uniform colour. Watch out for grub tunnels too. These are often warning indicators that the material is 'over the hill'.

If the cap is to be used in its entirety the best advice is to take it when it is dry and to tap it gently, gills pointing downwards, to remove any lodgers or dirt. If surplus material between the gills becomes waterlogged it is much more difficult to extract. Once this is done the upper surface of the cap can be washed and patted dry on a kitchen cloth. It is unnecessary to scrape or peel the cap: this does nothing for the palatability and will generally make the vegetable look less attractive. If you do not need to retain the cap in one piece cut it up into convenient slices. Large caps may need to be cubed but create chunks of no more than 4 cm across. Place the pieces in a colander and rinse them thoroughly under the tap, before drying them on a kitchen cloth. This way you will always remove far more undesirable intruders than if you attempt the operation when the cap is whole. Needless to say, the smaller the pieces the more efficient the process. Always ensure that the material is dry before cooking; it will retain texture far better than if it is swimming in water.

One of the great joys of mushroom cuisine is that fungi do not appeal merely on the yardstick of taste, but also that of shape, texture and colour. The connoisseur mushroom chefs place great emphasis on the artistic appearance which one kind of fungus will present when placed beside another or when put on the plate to accompany meat or fish. Thus pale creamy or white mushrooms like Pieds de Moutons (*Hydnum repandum*) tend to go with white meats like rabbit and chicken and with fish, unless one deliberately chooses to create a striking contrast, or unless a particular flavour suits the dish. Trompette de Mort (*Craterellus cornucopioides*) cooks to a blackish-grey but it is considered by many chefs to possess a subtle flavour which is second to none in complementing fish dishes.

It is an inevitability of human nature that the person experimenting with wild mushroom cookery for the first time will tread warily until confidence grows. In all probability the first tentative excursion with the pan is going to be a simple sauté in butter. There is nothing wrong with this basic approach and it is, in fact, one of the best methods of cooking mushrooms without disguising flavour and texture. A useful tip, though, is first to soften one or two chopped shallots on a moderate heat but being careful to avoid browning the butter. The shallots will enhance and complement the flavour of most fungi. Toss in the mushroom pieces, moving them constantly around the pan, and cook for no more than a minute and often, with delicate species, for no more than a few seconds.

Don't be afraid to incorporate those species which are suitable for use raw into fresh salads. Ceps, in particular, will make an attractive decorative effect if sliced thinly and arranged around the edge of the plate. One of David Chambers's favourite recipes incorporates Ceps with a piece of warm sautéed goose liver topping off the salad. *Lepista nuda* and *Lepiota procera* are equally suitable and, if you are lucky enough to find it, *Hygrocybe coccinea* will give a salad a bright and attractive orange red garnish.

If you want to savour wild mushrooms cooked and served to perfection in an infinite variety of delicious dishes then go to northern Italy. The city of Alba in Piedmont reeks with the indescribable aroma of truffles during the Tartufo Festival in October. At many of the restaurants of the area you will be obliged to tackle a stupendous but utterly delicious and irresistible fifteen-course meal (the *Pranzo Speciale*), incorporating fungi, and in particular the fabled white truffle *Tuber magnatum* with every course including the *dolce*. In France, the L'Ain region of eastern France and particularly the provincial town of Bourg en Bresse (of chicken fame) is an excellent place to get to know the delights of Ceps, morels and others. Perigord, the home of a celebrated black truffle, is also worth a visit. There, the locals gather in the dawn hours for a special kind of al fresco breakfast in the marketplaces. They eat mushroom omelettes off tin platters sluiced with red wine which is swirled and drunk directly from the plate.

The best way to store fungi for later use is to dry or pickle them. It is always better to collect mushrooms for storage in dry weather rather than when it is damp or raining. The first thing to bear in mind is that drying any quantity of fungi at home requires a lot of space and a patient understanding household! The larger specimens need to be sliced fairly thinly (about ½ cm) and then allowed to dry on sheets of clean paper in warm bedrooms, airing cupboards, in fact anywhere the air is dry and space is available. Small species like morels (*Morchella* spp.) and Fairy Ring Champignons (*Marasmius oreades*) are best threaded on cotton and hung across the room. The process can take about a week but the resultant shrivelled lumps often retain flavour and smell perfect. If there is a really hot dry spell in the autumn the job can be done out of doors, but in Britain this is probably out of the question in most years. Once dried, the material can be kept in sealed jars either in the form of convenient pieces, or as a powder, having been put through the blender.

Don't expect the flesh of dried mushrooms necessarily to return to its former glory when you reconstitute them before cooking. Rather think of the dried fungi in the same way as currants or dried apricots. The dried specimens are soaked in lukewarm salted water in a covered bowl and, generally speaking, they should be ready for use after about half an hour. One of the traditional methods in China which seems to work well is to soak first in lukewarm water then transfer to really hot water as if you were blanching. Either way the water is best discarded afterwards because it tends to become gritty.

The morels and some of the boletes, including *B. edulis*, are probably the best species for drying. *Sparassis*, incidentally, is excellent when chopped into small cubes and is also one of the few species which really does reconstitute to look more or less like the original fresh material.

Pickling is the obvious alternative to drying if you want to store wild mushrooms for any length of time. It is a time honoured art which is still familiar in Continental Europe and which seems to be gaining in popularity in Britain. Various methods work well but with differing results in terms of flavour and appearance. The best, but unfortunately also the most expensive technique, is to immerse the fungi in pure olive oil having first blanched them in hot brine for about 5 or 10 minutes (depending on size) and dried them thoroughly on clean kitchen paper towels. Alternatively you can place the caps and stalks into hot salted water as before and then mix them with about twice their own weight of small peeled onions or shallots. Then pack, a layer at a time, into a sterilized jar, adding pickling spices between the layers, seal and store. The flavour is less well retained but the method is more economical unless you have a very cheap source of virgin olive oil! It is important not to touch the material with your hands after blanching as the bacteria in your skin can do nasty things to it later. Always use a clean metal spoon.

Mushroom ketchup is also great fun and rather tasty. It is particularly suitable for those species which tend to go mushy. Cut the caps and stalks into smallish pieces and place them in a jar a layer at a time. Sift salt lightly between the layers. Seal the jar and leave for about a week in a warm dark place. Simmer the resultant mush gently for about 20 minutes and then rub it through a fine sieve with a wooden spoon. To each pint of ketchup add ½ oz of pickling spices and return the mixture to the heat for a further 20 minutes. Pour into serilized bottles and seal.

Generally speaking, mushrooms do not freeze well because of the amount of water they contain. It is useful to appreciate what happens in the freezing process. Ice crystals form inside the cells of the mushroom but when they thaw, they also expand and, in doing so, rupture all the tissues. It is this physical process which can turn what you hoped was going to emerge from the freezer looking pristine and crisp, into a sloppy mess! If you want to try freezing, use small specimens, preferably the drier species. Put them into a polythene bag, sealed to exclude as much air as possible, and freeze rapidly. When defrosting, speed is advisable. Never allow frozen mushrooms to thaw in their own time; instead drop the hard frozen specimens into boiling salted water for about a minute.

Further Reading

Buczacki, Stefan *New Generation Guide, Fungi of Britain and Europe*. Collins, 1989.

Carluccio, Antonio *A Passion for Mushrooms*. Pavilion, 1990.

Jordan, Michael *Mushroom Magic*. Elm Tree, 1989.

Phillips, Roger *Mushrooms and other Fungi of Great Britain and Europe*. Pan, 1981.

Index of Scientific Names

Index of Common Names